Freezer Paper
Quilting

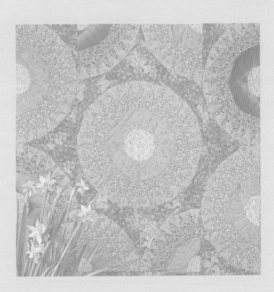

Linda Causee

LEISURE ARTS
the art of everyday living

Produced by

Production Team

Creative Directors: Rita Weiss and
Jean Leinhauser

Editorial Director: Linda Causee

Photography: Carol Wilson Mansfield

Technical Editing: Ann Harnden,
Christina Wilson

Book Design: Linda Causee

Pattern Testers: Hope Adams,
Shirley Cushing, Linda Ferguson,
Cathy Howell, Dawn Kallunki,
Ada LeClaire, and
Wanda MacLachlan

Machine Quilting: Faith Horsky

*The following companies supplied
their products for the projects in this
book:*

Fairfield Processing Corp.:
Machine 60/40 Blend®

Northcott Silks, Inc.:
Assorted fabrics used in *Framed
Stars* (page 34), *Irish Chain
Revisited* (page 44), *Take-Along
Ohio Star* (page 66), *Christmas
Stars & Angels* (page 82) and
Tulips in the Garden (page 88)

Published by Leisure Arts

the art of everyday living

© 2009 by Leisure Arts, Inc

Introduction

I thought freezer paper was just for wrapping meat; what a delusion!

Then a fellow quilter introduced me to its magical properties. We were both waiting in line to check our bags for our flights home after a quilt conference. I had one small bag; she had three very large ones. She was heading back home overseas, and I was certain that she had purchased every notion for sale at the conference.

"You certainly seem to have bought a lot of quilts," I joked.

"No," she said very sternly, "I didn't buy any quilts. These bags are filled with freezer paper. We can't get freezer paper back home. This should last me and my pals until I can return to the states to buy more."

And there in that crowded airport, she gave me my first lesson as to how freezer paper could become a quilter's best friend.

Since that day, I too have become fascinated with the power of freezer paper. The fact that it has a shiny side that will adhere to fabric when ironed, then easily removed, means that freezer paper has a multitude of wonderful possibilities. It makes appliqué easy; it eliminates the need to make all those paper patterns for foundation piecing; it makes hand piecing quicker and easier because there is no need to trace templates onto your fabric. Machine or hand quilting can be quicker and more precise when you apply your freezer paper quilting pattern onto your quilt.

And wonder of wonders, just when I thought I knew all of the uses for freezer paper, I find that freezer paper makes it really easy to transfer photos onto fabric. There's no telling what we might discover next!

So run down to the grocery store and buy a box of freezer paper, (or buy the sheets at your local quilt shop); get out your fabric, and start making quilts.

You'll never wrap meat again.

Contents

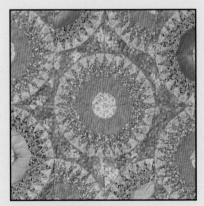

How to Use Freezer Paper to Make Quilts

WHAT IS FREEZER PAPER?

If you thought freezer paper was for wrapping meat, you are only partly right. But who would have thought that it could be such a wonderful tool for quilting. The great properties of freezer paper are that one side is dull on which you can draw and trace your patterns and the other side has a shiny, waxy surface that adheres to fabric when you iron it with a medium-hot iron. It is then easily removed when you are finished with the particular technique you are using.

You can find freezer paper in a roll made by Reynolds® at the supermarket in the aisle with the foil wrap, plastic wrap and plastic baggies. You can also buy freezer paper sheets by C. Jenkins at your local quilt shop. It comes in two sizes, 8^1/2" x 11" and 11" x 15".

FREEZER PAPER TECHNIQUES

Printing Photos on Fabric

Although purchased fabric sheets are easy to use, they can be very costly especially if you have several items to print onto fabric. To prepare your fabric for printing, you will need high-quality 100% cotton fabric, Bubble Jet Set 2000, a square plastic tub, rubber gloves, freezer paper, rotary cutter, mat and ruler, and Bubble Jet Rinse.

Note: *Bubble Jet Set 2000 and Bubble Jet Rinse can be purchased at your local quilt shop.*

Step 1: Use high-quality 100% cotton. The fabric should be at least 200 threads per inch. Cut the fabric into rectangles, 9" x 11^1/2" which is slightly larger than a 8^1/2" x 11" sheet of paper.

Step 2: Pour a little of the Bubble Jet Set 2000 into a square plastic tub. The Bubble Jet Set will allow the ink of your inkjet printer to bond permanently with your fabric.

Step 3: Place a fabric rectangle into the plastic tub. Wearing a pair of rubber gloves, push the fabric into the liquid until it is soaked through. Add another fabric rectangle, add a little more Bubble Jet set 2000 and thoroughly saturate the fabric. Continue this process until you have treated all the fabric needed for your project.

Step 4: Let the fabric air dry by hanging on a clothesline or lay the fabric on a table covered with plastic. Don't dry in the dryer. Pour any leftover Bubble Jet Set liquid back into the bottle for the next use.

Step 5: When the fabric rectangles are completely dry, iron to the shiny side of freezer paper. Be sure that there are no air bubbles between the fabric and freezer paper. Also, do not overheat the fabric and freezer paper or you will lose the bonding ability.

Step 6: Trim the sheets to 8^1/2" x 11". Be sure to use a sharp rotary cutter. Trim any loose threads hanging from the fabric edges.

Step 7: Change your printer settings to the highest DPI and the media type setting to high gloss photo paper. Print photos.

Step 8: Let the printed pages set at least 24 hours, then rinse with Bubble Jet Set Rinse. The rinsing step is important because it removes excess ink so the pictures don't run during subsequent washings. You do not need to heat set with an iron.

Foundation Piecing Method 1

One of the easiest and most accurate methods for creating perfect quilt squares is Foundation Piecing.

Freezer Paper as the Foundation

There are many choices that you can use as foundations for piecing. Plain copy paper is popular because of its availability. There are also special foundation sheets and other foundation materials on the market. Freezer paper, however, with its fusibility properties is the greatest choice for foundation piecing. You can print or trace the pattern on the dull side, and sew the fabrics onto the shiny side. As you sew and press, the fabrics will adhere to the freezer paper making the piecing a whole lot easier. As long as you use a small stitch, you will be able to tear the foundation easily after your quilt top is competely pieced.

Preparing the Foundation

Place freezer paper (shiny side down) over your chosen block and trace the block pattern. Use a ruler and a fine-line pencil or permanent marker, and make sure that all lines are straight. Sometimes short dashed lines or even dotted lines are easier to make. Be sure to copy all numbers. You will need to make a foundation for each block you are planning to use.

Hint: *Write the fabric color you will be using for each section on the pattern to make piecing easier.*

If you have a home inkjet printer/copier, you can copy the design straight from the book. Be sure the dull side of the freezer paper is the side that you are printing on. If you are unsure of whether to place the freezer paper sheets shiny side up or down in your printer, run a test sheet by placing a mark on a piece of copy paper, printing out the sheet and checking which side the mark is on. **Note:** *Copy patterns for your personal use only.* Purchase 8 1/2" x 11" freezer paper sheets by C. Jenkins or cut sheets from the roll made by manufacturers such as Reynolds®.

Important: *Do not use freezer paper in a laser printer. The waxy surface will melt due to the heat generated while printing.*

Since the copy machine might slightly alter the measurements of the block, make certain that you copy each block from the original pattern.

You can also scan the block if you have a home scanner and then print out the required number of blocks onto freezer paper.

Cutting the Fabric

In foundation piecing, you do not have to cut perfect shapes!

You can, therefore, use odd pieces of fabric: squares, strips, rectangles. The one thing you must remember, however, is that every piece must be at least 1/4" larger on all sides than the space it is going to cover. Strips and squares are easy—just measure the length and width of the needed space and add 1/2" all around. Cut your strip to that measurement. Triangles, however, can be a bit tricky. In that case, measure the widest point of the triangle and cut your fabric about 1/2" to 1" wider.

Other Supplies for Foundation Piecing

You will need a cleaned and oiled sewing machine, paper scissors, fabric scissors, a small craft iron or travel iron and a small ironing surface. **Hint:** *Use a piece of cardboard covered with a towel for your ironing surface.*

Before beginning to sew your actual block, determine the proper stitch length. Use a piece of the freezer paper you are planning to use for the foundation and draw a straight line on it. Set your machine so that it sews with a fairly short stitch (about 20 stitches per inch). Sew along the line. If you can tear the paper apart with ease, you are sewing with the right length. You don't want to sew with such a short stitch that the paper falls apart by itself.

Using a Pattern

The numbers on the block show the order in which the pieces are to be placed and sewn on the base. It is extremely important that you follow the numbers; otherwise the entire process won't work. If the block is made up of several sections, the sections will be labeled with letters of the alphabet. You will need to cut apart the sections and piece them individually, then sew the sections together in alphabetical order.

Making the Block

The important thing to remember about making a foundation block is that the fabric pieces go on the unmarked side of the foundation while you sew on the printed side. The finished blocks are a mirror image of the original pattern.

Step 1: Hold the foundation up to a light source - even a window pane - with the unmarked side facing you. Find the space marked 1 on the unmarked side and place the fabric right side up on the unmarked side on Space 1, making certain that the fabric overlaps at least $1/4"$ on all sides of space 1. Iron fabric in place with a small craft iron. (**Diagram 1**)

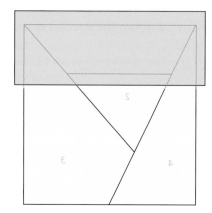

Diagram 1

Step 2: Fold the foundation along the line between Space 1 and Space 2. Cut the fabric so that it is $1/4"$ from the fold. (**Diagram 2**)

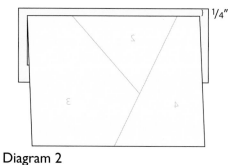

Diagram 2

Step 3: With right sides together, place Fabric Piece 2 on Fabric Piece 1, making sure that the edge of Piece 2 is even with the just-trimmed edge of Piece 1. (**Diagram 3**)

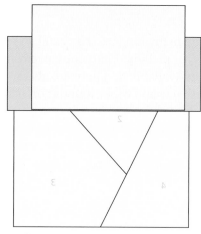

Diagram 3

Step 4: To make certain that Piece 2 will cover Space 2, fold the fabric piece back along the line between Space 1 and Space 2. (**Diagram 4**)

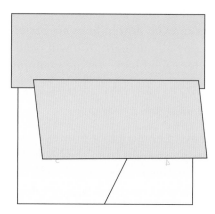

Diagram 4

Step 5: With the marked side of the foundation facing up, place the piece on the sewing machine, holding both Piece 1 and Piece 2 in place. Sew along the line between Space 1 and Space 2. (**Diagram 5**)

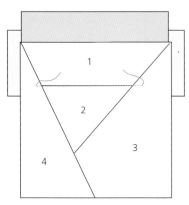

Diagram 5

Note: *If you use a small stitch, it will be easier to remove the paper later. Start sewing about two or three stitches before the beginning of the line and end your sewing two or three stitches beyond the line. This will allow the stitching to be held in place by the next round of stitching rather than by backstitching.*

Step 6: Turn the work over and open Piece 2. Press with a small craft or travel iron. (**Diagram 6**)

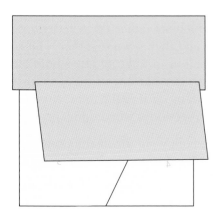

Diagram 6

Step 7: Turning the work so that the marked side is on top, fold the foundation forward along the line between Space 1+2 and Space 3. Trim about ⅛" to ¼" from the fold. It is easier to trim the paper if you pull the paper away from the stitching. (**Diagram 7**)

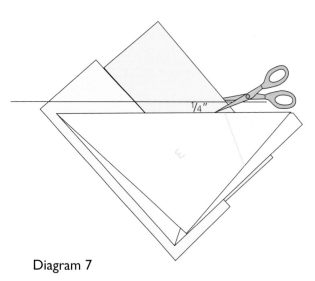

Diagram 7

Step 8: Place Fabric #3 right side down even with the just-trimmed edge. (**Diagram 8**)

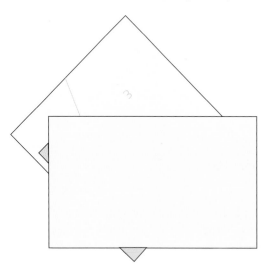

Diagram 8

Step 9: Turn the block over to the marked side and sew along the line between Space 1+2 and Space 3. (**Diagram 9**)

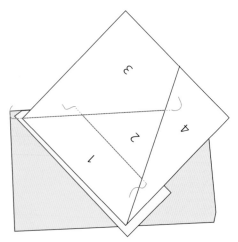

Diagram 9

Step 10: Turn the work over, open Piece 3 and press the seam with a small craft or travel iron. (**Diagram 10**)

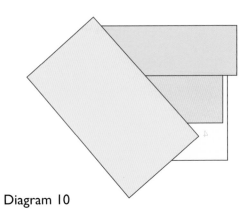

Diagram 10

Step 11: In the same way you have added the other pieces, add Piece #4 to complete this block. (**Diagram 11**)

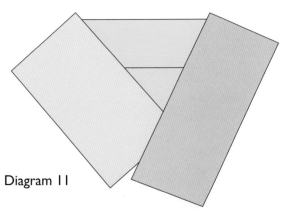

Diagram 11

Step 12: Trim the fabric ¹/₄" from the edge of the foundation. The foundation-pieced block is completed. (**Diagram 12**)

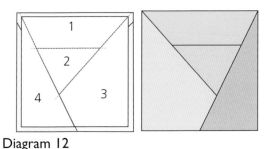

Diagram 12

After you have finished sewing a block, don't immediately remove the paper. Since you are often piecing with tiny bits of fabric, grainline is never a factor. Therefore, some of the pieces may have been cut on the bias and may have a tendency to stretch. You can eliminate any problem with distortion by keeping the paper in place until all of the blocks have been sewn together. If, however, you want to remove the paper, staystitch along the outer edge of the block to help keep the block in shape.

Sewing Multiple Sections

Some blocks in foundation piecing, such as those in *Blazing Blossoms*, page 104 and *Baxter the Boxer*, page 124, are created with two or more sections. These sections, which are indicated by letters, are individually pieced and then sewn together. The cutting line for these sections is indicated by a bold blue line. Before you start to make any of these multi-section blocks, begin by cutting the foundation pattern apart so that each section is worked independently.

Step 1: Following the instructions above for Making the Block, complete each section.

Hint: *For patterns with many sections such as* Baxter the Boxer, *page 124 and* My Angel the Pug, *page 110, piece sections in alphabetical order. For example, piece sections A and B individually, then piece those two sections together. Piece section C, then sew section C to sections A/B. Continue sewing until the entire quilt is finished.*

Step 2: Place the sections right sides together. Pin the corners of the top section to the corners of the bottom section. (**Diagram 13**)

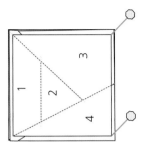

Diagram 13

Step 3: When you are certain that the pieces are aligned correctly, sew the two sections together using the regular stitch length on the sewing machine. (**Diagram 14**)

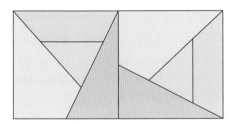

Diagram 14

Step 4: Press the sections open, then continue sewing the sections until block is completed. (**Diagram 15**)

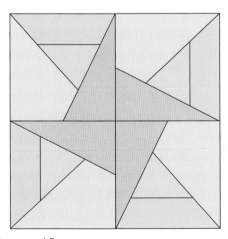

Diagram 15

What You Don't Want to Forget

1. Start stitching two or three stitches before the start of the stitching line and finish your stitching two or three stitches beyond the end.

2. Use a short stitch (about 20 stitches per inch) for paper foundations to make it easier to remove the paper. If the paper falls apart as you sew, your stitches are too short.

3. Iron each seam and fabric piece in place as you finish it. Use a small craft or travel iron.

4. Stitching which goes from a space into another space will not interfere with adding additional fabric pieces.

5. Remember to trim all seam allowances at least $^1/_4$".

6. When sewing points, start from the wide end and sew towards the point.

7. Unless you plan to use it only once in the block, it is a good idea to stay away from directional prints in foundation piecing.

8. When cutting pieces for foundation piecing, never worry about the grainline.

9. Always remember to sew on the marked side, placing the fabric on the unmarked side.

10. Follow the numerical order, or it won't work.

11. Once you have finished making a block, do not remove the paper until the entire quilt has been finished unless you staystitch around the outside of the block.

12. Be sure that the ink you use to make your foundation is permanent so it doesn't smear onto your fabric.

Foundation Piecing Method 2

This method is similar to Method 1 except that you will not be sewing on the freezer paper. Instead, you will sew next to folded freezer paper. When your block is complete you will be able to re-use the pattern at least three or four more times.

Step 1: Cut pieces of freezer paper, 8$\frac{1}{2}$" x 11" or use purchased pre-cut sheets at your local quilt shop.

Step 2: Using an inkjet copier, copy as many patterns as you will need for your project. You will be able to use each pattern at least three to five times before it loses its ability to adhere to fabric.

Important: *Use an inkjet copier only. The heat generated by laser copiers will cause the waxy side of the freezer paper to melt.*

Step 3: Position Fabric Piece 1 right side up on shiny (unmarked) side of freezer paper pattern; fuse in place using a small craft or travel iron to make fusing easier. (**Diagram 16**)

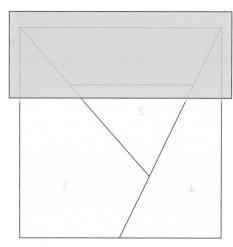

Diagram 16

Step 4: Fold freezer paper back along line between Spaces 1 and 2. Place on a cutting mat and using a rotary cutter and acrylic ruler, trim fabric $\frac{1}{4}$" from folded edge. (**Diagram 17**)

Diagram 17

Step 5: With the foundation still folded, place Space 2 fabric right sides together with Space 1 fabric. Fabric 2 will be on the bottom. **Hint:** *Double check fabric piece so that it will cover Space 2 completely.*

Step 6: Stitch next to fold, using a regular stitch length and being careful not to catch paper in your stitching. (**Diagram 18**)

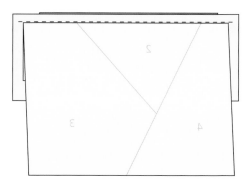

Diagram 18

Hint: *Since the shiny side of the freezer paper foundation will be directly under your presser foot when sewing, you may need to place a strip of paper directly under the presser foot on top of the freezer paper. The strip should only be wide enough to fit under your presser foot and be sure the paper is positioned so that it does not get caught in your stitching.*

Step 7: Unfold pattern and fold Fabric Piece 2 open and fuse in place. (**Diagram 19**)

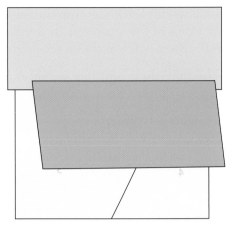

Diagram 19

Step 8: Fold freezer paper along line between Spaces 2 and 3. Place on a cutting mat and using a rotary cutter and acrylic ruler, trim ¹/4" from fold. (**Diagram 20**)

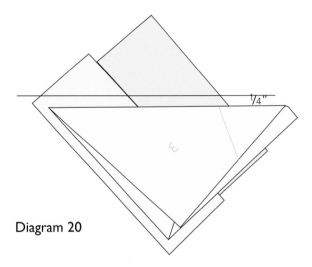

Diagram 20

Step 9: Keeping the foundation folded, place Space 3 fabric right sides together with fabric 1/2. Space 3 fabric will be on the bottom. Stitch next to fold. (**Diagram 21**)

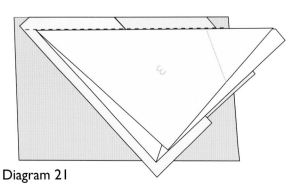

Diagram 21

Step 10: Fold fabric open and iron in place. (**Diagram 22**)

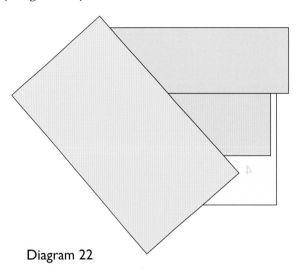

Diagram 22

Step 11: Continue sewing in this manner until block (or section) is completely pieced. (**Diagram 23**)

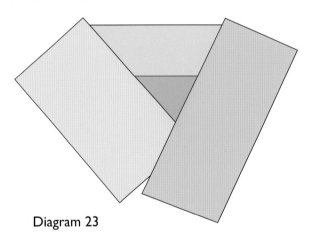

Diagram 23

Step 12: Trim outside edge of block or pattern ¹/₄" from edge of freezer paper foundation. (**Diagram 24**)

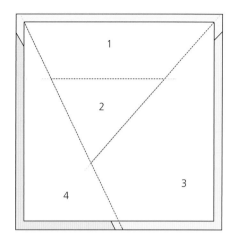

Diagram 24

Step 13: If you want to remove the paper before sewing your quilt top together, staystitch the block next to the outside edge of the pattern. (**Diagram 25**) Remove freezer paper pattern.

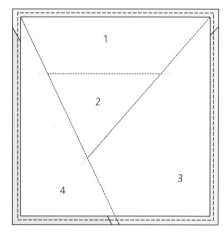

Diagram 25

Freezer Paper Appliqué

Hand Appliqué

Supplies

For hand appliqué there are a few basic supplies that you will need—many of which will most likely be found in your sewing basket.

Needles: Use a needle that is comfortable for you to work with. It can be a sharp—general use needle, a between—used mainly for hand quilting or even a straw needle—extra fine sewing needle. As long as it is sharp and easy for you to handle, it will work for appliqué.

Thread: Use 100 percent cotton thread that matches the color of the piece you are appliquéing. A thin-weight thread such as #60 is recommended.

Pins: Use thin, sharp pins that are short in length to help keep your thread from getting tangled.

Freezer paper: Use freezer paper—found in most grocery stores—for the templates used in your appliqué.

Thimble: Use a well-fitting thimble when you appliqué.

Iron: Use an iron to press seam allowances onto freezer paper. The small craft irons available today are wonderful to use.

Freezer Paper Appliqué Technique

Step 1: Trace pattern pieces onto the dull side of freezer paper. Be sure to trace each piece the number of times that pattern will be used in your project. Cut freezer paper along drawn lines. (**Diagram 26**)

Diagram 26

Step 2: Place freezer paper patterns shiny side down onto wrong side of fabric; fuse in place. Cut out fabric about ¹/₄" from the edge of the freezer paper. (**Diagram 27**)

Diagram 27

Step 3: Clip seam allowances along inside curves. Never clip outside curves. (**Diagram 28**)

Diagram 28

Step 4: Fold edges over freezer paper and using a hot iron, press seam allowance. (**Diagram 29**)

Diagram 29

Step 5: Prepare all appliqué pieces in the same manner. Do not remove freezer paper.

Step 6: Cut background fabric the size specified in the project directions; press. For placement guides, fold background in half, then in quarters. (**Diagram 30**)

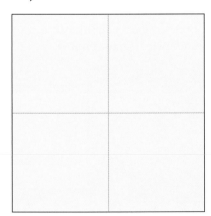

Diagram 30

Step 7: Place background on a flat ironing surface. Using the photograph and/or placement guide, position the first piece on background fabric.

Continue placing appliqué pieces until a pleasing arrangement is achieved. (**Diagram 31**)

Diagram 31

Step 8: Baste or pin pieces in place.

Step 9: Stitch edges of appliqués using matching thread and an invisible stitch. (**Diagram 32**)

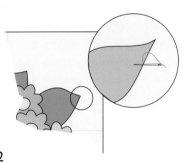

Diagram 32

Step 10: When all pieces are appliquéd in place, carefully make slits in the background fabric and re-move freezer paper. Cut away fabric about $1/4$" from stitching lines. (**Diagram 33**)

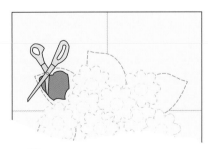

Diagram 33

Two-Layer Designs

Some appliqué pieces such as the flowers in *My Flower Garden*, page 20, are made up of two layers. It is best to appliqué the top layer onto the bottom first before appliquéing to background fabric. Place the top (center) piece onto the Petal piece and appliqué in place. Turn Petal piece over, make a small slit and remove freezer paper and trim backing ¼" from stitching. (**Diagram 34**)

Diagram 34

Easy Appliqué

For easy appliqué, you will need to use paper-backed fusible web. There are many different paper-backed fusible products on the market today. Each has its own unique characteristics that will help you decide which to use when making a quilt. Always be sure to follow the manufacturer's directions as each product differs greatly.

The *Mini Quilt Greeting Cards*, page 56, were made using the lightweight paper-backed fusible web, HeatnBond Lite®. This will enable you to use a machine zigzag to appliqué the edges. Using a heavy-weight brand will cause your needle to gum up and possibly break.

Step 1: Trace all the pattern(s) that you will need for your project onto the paper side of the fusible web. Rough cut the pattern shapes.
Hint: *Trace patterns that will use the same fabric together. For example, if you have several leaves, trace them together on the fusible web, then cut out the entire section of leaves. Don't cut out leaves one at a time.*

Step 2: Position fusible web pattern with paper side up onto wrong side of fabric; fuse in place with hot iron. Cut out fabric shapes along drawn lines.

Note: *Refer to manufacturer's directions for heating setting and pressing time for the product you are using.*

Step 3: Position the fusible appliqué pieces onto background fabric as shown in the individual project instructions. Fuse pieces into place following manufacturer's directions.

Machine Appliqué

Using a machine zigzag or blanket stitch and matching or invisible thread, stitch along all raw edges of appliqué. You may want to practice on another piece of fabric to see which zigzag width and length works best for you.

Appliqué with Fusible Interfacing

Using fusible interfacing can make the appliqué process easier by giving smooth, turned-under raw edges. Also, the pieces to be appliquéd can be fused in place for sewing. You will need freezer paper and lightweight fusible interfacing.

Step 1: Trace pattern onto dull side of freezer paper. Cut out along drawn line. (**Diagram 35**)

Diagram 35

Step 2: Press freezer paper pattern on wrong side of chosen fabric. (**Diagram 36**)

Diagram 36

Note: *You do not have to cut out exact pattern shape yet.*

Step 3: Place fabric right sides together with bumpy (fusible) side of interfacing. Sew along entire edge of appliqué pattern using a short stitch. (**Diagram 37**)

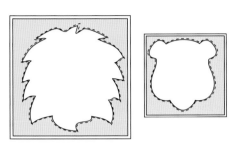

Diagram 37

Step 4: Trim ⅛" to ¼" from stitching line. (**Diagram 38**)

Diagram 38

Step 5: Cut a slit in center of fusible interfacng. (**Diagram 39**)

Diagram 39

Step 6: Turn appliqué right side out through slit. (**Diagram 40**)

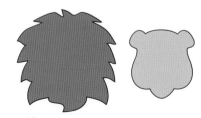

Diagram 40

Step 7: Place appliqué on background fabric; press with an iron to fuse in place. (**Diagram 41**)

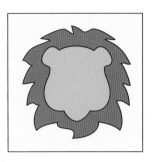

Diagram 41

Writing on Fabric

There are many times that you may want to write on fabric. You will need a permanent fabric marker and freezer paper to make the writing easier. *The Finishing Touch* quilt labels, pages 140 to 149, are made according to the project instruction. Then press a piece of freezer paper, shiny side down on the wrong side of the quilt label. Turn the label over and write the quilt information that you would like to add to the quilt onto the right side of the label. Once you are done writing, remove the freezer paper and continue with the project.

For the *Mini Quilt Greeting Cards*, pages 56 to 65, make the project tops according to the project instructions. Fuse a piece of freezer paper shiny side down to the wrong side of the project backing; turn over and write your message onto the fabric. Remove the freezer paper then layer, quilt and bind according to Finishing Your Quilt, pages 156 to 159.

Hand Piecing

Using freezer paper templates makes hand piecing easier and quicker than tracing plastic or cardboard templates onto your fabric.

Step 1. Draw or copy templates onto dull side of freezer paper. Make a set of templates for every 3 or 4 blocks.

Note: *Templates are the finished size so they do not include the seam allowance. The seam allowance is added when cutting out the fabric.*

Step 2. Cut out templates along drawn lines. (**Diagram 42**)

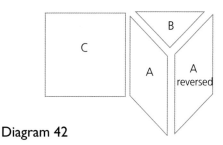

Diagram 42

Step 3. Fuse freezer paper templates to wrong side of desired fabric; cut out ¼" from edge of freezer paper. (**Diagram 43**)

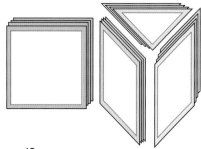

Diagram 43

Step 4. Place two diamond shapes (with freezer paper still fused) right sides together. Using a needle and thread, sew along edge of freezer paper. Be sure to knot thread at each end. (**Diagram 44**)

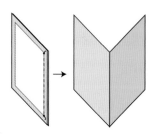

Diagram 44

Step 5. Sew the triangle in between the two diamonds. Sew one short edge of the triangle to a diamond, beginning at the inner point and working toward the outer edge. (**Diagram 45**)

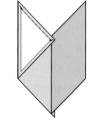

Diagram 45

Step 6: Repeat with the adjacent short edge of the triangle and the other diamond. (**Diagram 46**) Repeat for three more units.

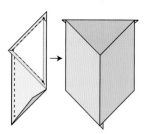

Diagram 46

Step 7: Sew units from step 6 together in pairs. (**Diagram 47**)

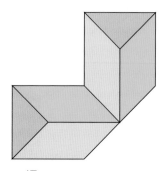

Diagram 47

Step 8: Sew pairs of units together. (**Diagram 48**)

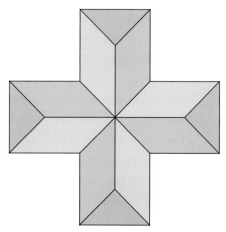

Diagram 48

Step 9: To complete the block, sew squares to each corner in the same manner as sewing the triangles, working from the inside point to the outside edge. (**Diagram 49**)

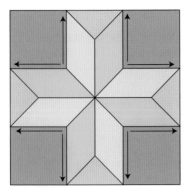

Diagram 49

Note: *If you will be sewing the blocks together by hand, you need to keep the freezer paper templates attached so that you have the edges to use as guidelines for sewing. If you will be piecing by machine, be sure to square up the blocks and make sure that all blocks are the same size. You can then remove the freezer paper and sew the blocks together by machine using a ¹/₄" seam allowance.*

Freezer Paper Quilting Patterns

Freezer paper can be a great tool for quilting motifs on your quilt. It can be especially useful when you need to trace a quilting design on a dark fabric such as on the *Irish Chain Revisited*, page 44.

Step 1: Trace the quilting design onto the dull side of the freezer paper. Cut out along drawn line. Make enough patterns for your entire quilt remembering that you can use each pattern at least three or four times.

Step 2: Layer and baste your quilt referring to Attaching the Batting and Backing, page 156. Quilt in the ditch between blocks and borders (page 156).

Step 3: Iron freezer paper patterns where desired on your quilt, starting in the center. (**Diagram 50**)

Diagram 50

Hint: *Iron only a few patterns at a time in the center to avoid freezer paper from becoming loose.*

Step 4: Using free form machine quilting (pages 156 to 157), quilt along edge of freezer paper patterns making sure you don't quilt through the paper. (**Diagram 51**)

Diagram 51

Step 5: Once you have completed the center section, remove the freezer paper patterns. Iron patterns to another section of the quilt and quilt along edge of freezer paper. Peel off freezer paper patterns. (**Diagram 52**)

Diagram 52

Step 6: Continue in this manner until entire quilt is quilted.

My Flower Garden

If you love beautiful flowers, but don't enjoy getting your hands dirty in the garden, you can still have your very own flower garden by putting your flowers on a quilt. This quilt is actually hand appliquéd, but using freezer paper patterns makes the work easy.

Freezer Paper Technique
Freezer Paper Appliqué (pages 14 to 17)

Approximate Size
39" x 39"

Block Size
9" x 9" finished

Materials
1^1/$_2$ yards light green (background, first border)
1 yard dark green print (Scallops, second border, binding)
Assorted scraps for flowers, leaves and stems
1^1/$_4$ yards backing
Batting
Freezer paper
Fabric marking pen or pencil

Patterns
Carnations (page 24)
Tulips (page 25)
Pink Flowers (page 26)
Asters (page 27)
Blue Flower (page 28)
Iris (page 29)
Pansy (page 30)
Sweet Peas (page 31)
Rose (page 32)
Scallop (page 33)

Cutting
Blocks

Note: *See Freezer Paper Appliqué, pages 14 to 16, to cut appliqué patterns.*
9 squares, 9^1/$_2$" x 9^1/$_2$", light green

Finishing
4 strips, 3^1/$_2$"-wide, light green (first border)
4 strips, 3^1/$_2$"-wide, dark geen print (second border)
4 strips, 2^1/$_2$"-wide, binding

Instructions

Blocks

1. Fold background square in half, then in half again to divide the block in four sections.

2. To make placement of appliqué easier, draw a line $^1/_4$" from each edge of the right side of the light green $9^1/_2$" background square; then, trace entire flower onto right side of block. (**Diagram 1**) Repeat for all blocks.

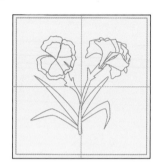

Diagram 1

3. Trace pattern pieces onto paper side of freezer paper. Cut out pieces along drawn lines.

4. Referring to Freezer Paper Appliqué, page 14, fuse the freezer paper patterns onto wrong side of fabrics for flowers and leaves. Cut out patterns about $^1/_4$" from edge of freezer paper.

5. Press edges over freezer paper.

6. Appliqué floral pieces to each $9^1/_2$" background square as shown on pattern pages 24 to 32. Appliqué Scallops (page 33) along each edge of blocks. (**Diagram 2**)

7. Remove freezer paper referring to step 10 of Freezer Paper Appliqué on page 15.

Diagram 2

Finishing

1. Sew blocks together in three rows of three blocks. (**Diagram 3**)

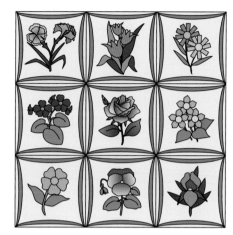

Diagram 3

2. Measure quilt lengthwise. Cut two $3^1/_2$"-wide light green strips to that length. Sew to sides of quilt.

3. Measure quilt crosswise. Cut two $3^1/_2$"-wide light green strips to that length. Sew to top and bottom of quilt.

4. Appliqué Scallops to border. (**Diagram 4**)

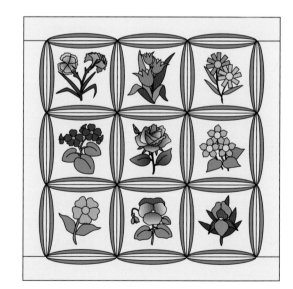

Diagram 4

5. Repeat steps 2 and 3 for second border using $3\frac{1}{2}$"-wide dark green print strips.

6. Refer to Finishing Your Quilt, pages 156 to 159, to complete your quilt.

My Flower Garden **Quilt Layout**

Carnations

Tulips

Asters

Blue Flower

Iris

Pansy

Sweet Peas

Rose

Scallop

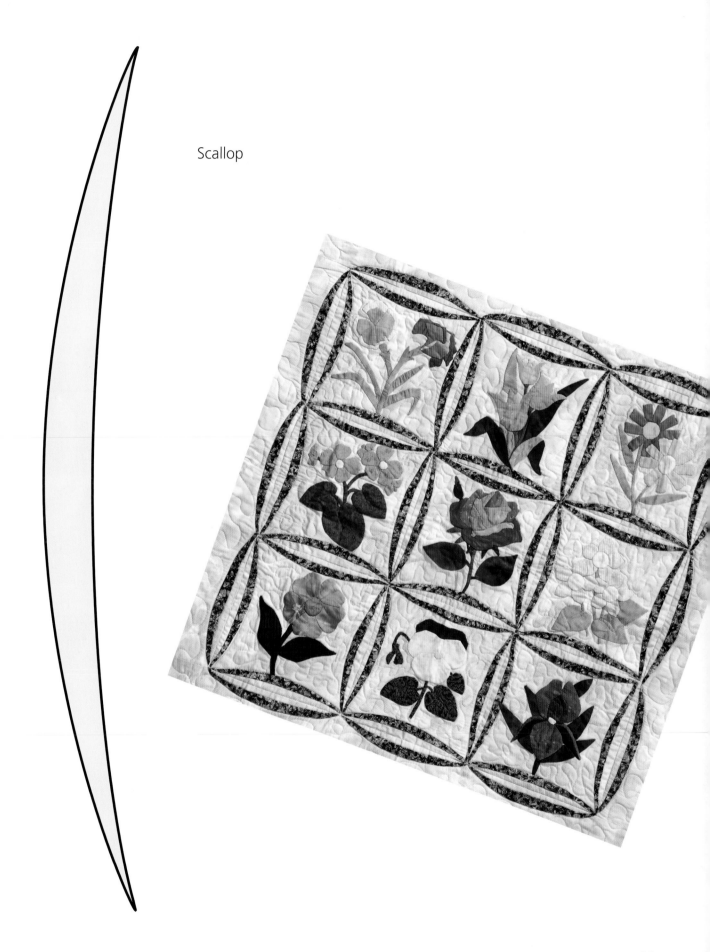

Framed Stars

When you look at this quilt, don't be fooled into thinking that it's too difficult. By using freezer paper foundation piecing, you'll be able to create this quilt in no time. Amaze your friends and relatives with your prowess!

Freezer Paper Technique
Foundation Piecing (pages 7 to 14)

Approximate Size
52 1/2" x 66 1/2"

Block Size
7" x 7" finished

Materials
1 yard dark blue fabric
1 1/4 yards purple fabric (includes first border)
1 yard medium blue/purple fabric
1 yard pastel multi-colored fabric
1 yard green/blue fabric
1 yard red fabric
1 yard coral pink fabric
1 yard peach multi-colored fabric (second border)
1/2 yard binding
1 yard backing
Batting
Freezer paper

Pattern
Quarter Star (page 39)

Cutting
Note: *Refer to Foundation Piecing Methods 1 and 2, pages 7 to 14, for cutting pieces. You will need the following pieces.*

Block 1
32 Shape 1, purple
32 Shape 2, green/blue
32 Shape 3, coral pink
32 Shape 4, red
8 Shape 5, dark blue
24 Shape 5, green/blue
32 Shape 6, pastel multi-colored
32 Shape 7, medium blue/purple
32 Shape 8, red

Block 2

16 Shape 1, purple
16 Shape 2, dark blue
16 Shape 3, coral pink
16 Shape 4, red
16 Shape 5, dark blue
16 Shape 6, pastel multi-colored
16 Shape 7, medium blue/purple
16 Shape 8, red

Block 3

32 Shape 1, purple
32 Shape 2, dark blue
32 Shape 3, coral pink
32 Shape 4, red
24 Shape 5, dark blue
8 Shape 5, green/blue
32 Shape 6, pastel multi-colored
32 Shape 7, medium blue/purple
32 Shape 8, red

Block 4

16 Shape 1, purple
16 Shape 2, dark blue
16 Shape 3, coral pink
16 Shape 4, red
8 Shape 5, dark blue
8 Shape 5, green/blue
16 Shape 6, pastel multi-colored
16 Shape 7, medium blue/purple
16 Shape 8, red

Finishing

4 strips, $2^{1}/4$"-wide, purple (first border)
4 strips, 4"-wide, peach multi-colored (second border)
4 strips, $2^{1}/2$"-wide, blue/green (binding)

Instructions

Blocks

Note: *Refer to Foundation Piecing Methods 1 and 2, pages 7 to 14 to decide which method you would like to use.*

1. Print or trace Quarter Star patterns onto dull side of freezer paper. (**Diagram 1**) You will need 48 patterns if using Foundation Piecing Method 1 and about 12 patterns for Method 2.

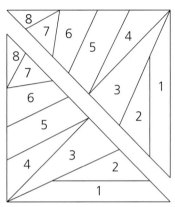

Diagram 1

2. Make 48 Quarter Star blocks referring to **Diagram 2**. You will need 12 Block A, 24 Block B, eight block C and four Block D.

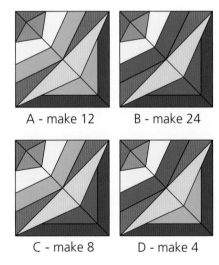

A - make 12   B - make 24

C - make 8   D - make 4

Diagram 2

3. Make four Star block 1, two Star block 2, four Star block 3 and two Star block 4. (**Diagram 3**)

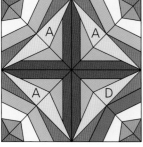
Block 1 - make 4

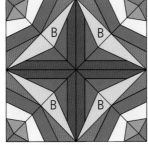
Block 2 - make 2

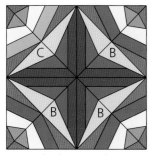
Block 3 - make 4

Block 4 - make 2

Diagram **3**

Finishing

1. Position Star blocks 1, 2, 3, and 4 in four rows of three blocks each. (**Diagram 4**)

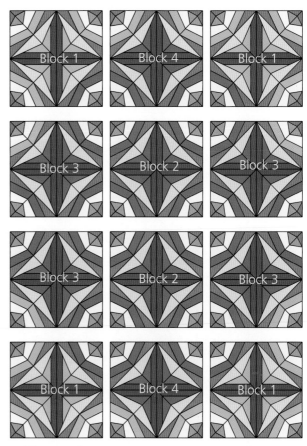
Diagram **4**

2. Sew blocks together in rows, then sew rows together.

3. Measure quilt lengthwise. Sew and cut 2$\frac{1}{4}$"-wide purple strips to that length. Sew to sides of quilt. Measure quilt crosswise. Sew and cut 2$\frac{1}{4}$"-wide purple strips to that length. Sew to top and bottom of quilt.

4. Repeat step 3 for second border using 4"-wide peach multi-colored strips.

5. Refer to Finishing Your Quilt, pages 156 to 159, to complete your quilt.

Framed Stars Quilt Layout

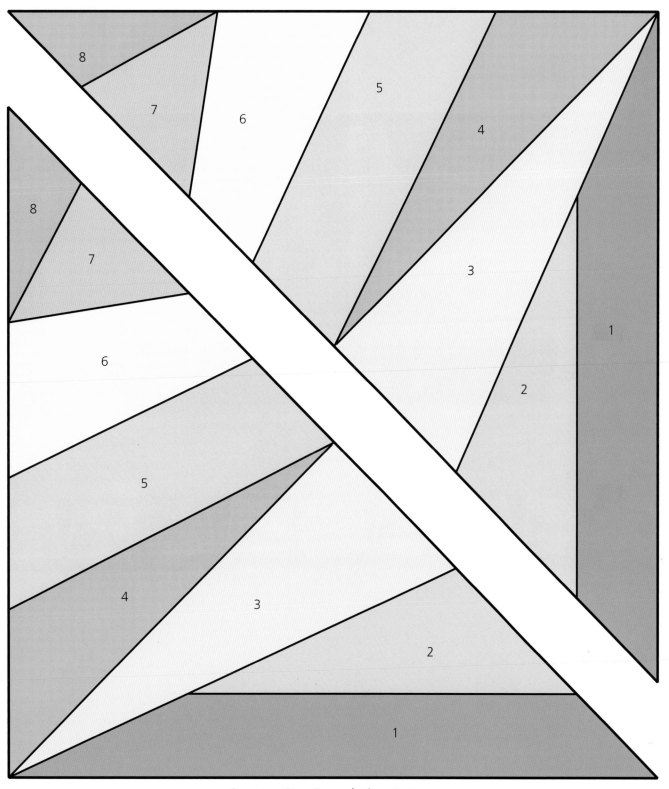

Quarter Star Foundation Pattern

Cruising to Alaska

What a wonderful way to remember a family cruise through an awesome glacier! All the fellow cruisers peek out through the windows of the ship while the borders of the quilt are filled with photos taken on the trip. Because freezer paper makes it easy to print the photos on fabric, the quilt is so easy to make.

Freezer Paper Technique
Printing Photos on Fabric (page 6)

Approximate Size
42" x 26"

Materials
$^5/_8$ yard blue 1 (sky fabric)
$^1/_8$ yard blue 2 (water fabric)
$^1/_2$ yard white/blue (glacier fabric)
$^3/_8$ yard gray fabric (ship)
$^1/_8$ yard black fabric (ship)
Scrap red fabric (ship)
$^1/_2$ yard white fabric (photos)
1 yard dark blue fabric (border and binding)
$1 ^1/_2$ yards backing
Batting
Freezer paper (enough to print photos)
Lightweight paper-backed fusible web
Small piece of clear template plastic
Permanent marking pen
Invisible monofilament thread

Pattern
$1 ^1/_2$"-diameter Circle (page 43)

Cutting
Quilt Center
1 Rectangle, $34 ^1/_2$" x $18 ^1/_2$", blue 1
1 Rectangle, 34" x 4", blue 2
1 Rectangle, 34" x 13", white/blue
1 Rectangle, $29 ^1/_2$" x $7 ^1/_2$", gray
1 Rectangle, $17 ^1/_2$" x 3", gray
1 Rectangle, $28 ^1/_2$" x $3 ^1/_2$", black
7 Rectangles, $1 ^1/_4$" x $^1/_2$", black
2 Rectangles, $1 ^1/_2$" x $2 ^1/_2$", red
6 Circles, $1 ^1/_2$"-diameter, black (or use photos)

Finishing
2 strips, $4 ^1/_2$" x $18 ^1/_2$", dark blue (side borders)
2 strips, $4 ^1/_2$" x $42 ^1/_2$", dark blue (top and bottom borders)
4 strips, $2 ^1/_2$"-wide, dark blue (binding)

Instructions

Preparing Photos

1. Refer to Printing Photos on Fabric, page 6, to prepare fabric and print photos onto fabric. **Note:** *The photographed quilt uses photos along the top and bottom borders, but you can use as many photos that can fit along the entire border of your quilt. The photos should be about 3½" x 3" so that they fit within the border. For the Circle photos, print out people photos so that the faces fit within a 1½" circle.*

2. Once photos are printed onto fabric, fuse to paper-backed fusible web.

3. For Circle photos, trace 1½"-diameter Circle onto template plastic using permanent marking pen; cut out. Position Circle template on face photos so that the portion of the photo that you want to use is within the Circle; trace Circle using a fabric pen or pencil. Cut out photos along drawn lines.

4. For remaining photos, trim about ⅛" to ¼" from edge of photo.

Quilt Center

1. Fuse paper-backed fusible web onto back of glacier rectangle. **Hint:** *If you do not want the stiffness of the fusible web on your quilt, fuse 1"-wide strips along side and bottom edges of glacier rectangle; fuse a 3"-wide strip of fusible web along top edge.*

2. Place glacier fabric right side up on cutting mat. Using your rotary cutter, cut a wavy edge off the top edge within the 3" strip of fusible web. (**Diagram 1**)

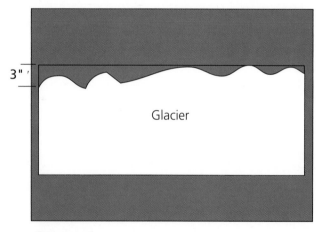

Diagram 1

3. For ship, fuse paper-backed fusible web to wrong side of gray, black and red rectangles, then cut gray and black rectangles according to **Diagram 2**.

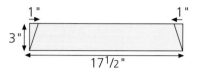

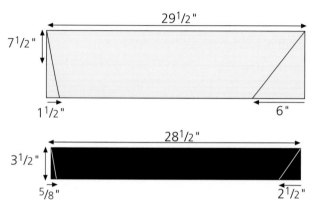

Diagram 2

4. Fuse paper-backed fusible web onto wrong side of water rectangle. Place on cutting mat and using rotary cutter, trim a gentle curve along top edge.

5. On ironing surface, position glacier onto sky rectangle about 3½" from the top. Then place all ship pieces (except windows) on glacier with bottom of ship even with bottom of glacier. Place water rectangle along bottom edge of sky rectangle. Fuse all pieces carefully in place. (**Diagram 3**)

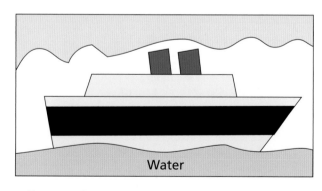

Diagram 3

6. Fuse photo Circles along black portion and small black rectangular windows to upper gray portion of ship. (**Diagram 4**)

Note: If you do not want to use photos, cut out and fuse white Circles to ship.

Diagram 4

7. Using invisible monofilament thread, machine zigzag along raw edges of glacier, ship, water and photos.

Finishing

1. Sew a 4¹/₂" x 18¹/₂" dark blue strip to sides of quilt top. Sew 4¹/₂" x 42¹/₂" dark blue strips to top and bottom.

2. Fuse photos along border referring to photograph or use your own arrangement.

3. Refer to Finishing Your Quilt, pages 156 to 159, to complete your quilt.

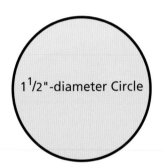

1¹/₂"-diameter Circle

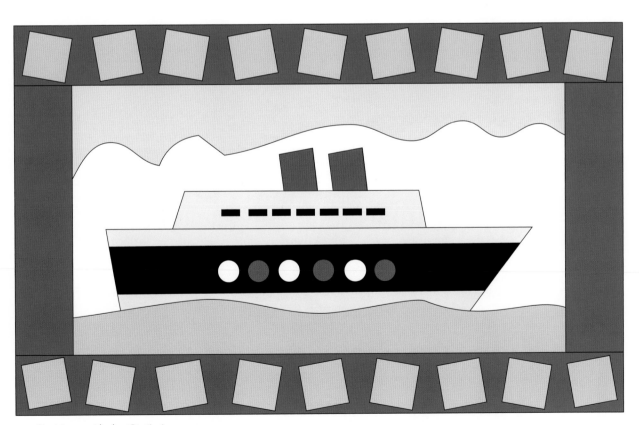

Cruising to Alaska **Quilt Layout**

Irish Chain Revisited

Here is the traditional Irish Chain with gold, rust and black chains crossing diagonally across a queen-size quilt. Add the finishing touch by using the freezer paper quilting patterns to quilt a star flower motif in the plain alternating blocks.

Freezer Paper Technique
Freezer Paper Quilting Patterns (page 19)

Approximate Size
86" x 114"

Block Size
14" x 14" finished

Materials
1 yard gold print
1 yard rust print 1
1 yard rust print 2
3 yards white/gold print (includes first border)
3 yards black print
3 yards black/rust print (includes second border)
1 yard binding
$7^{1}/_{2}$ yards backing
Batting
Freezer paper

Pattern
Flower Quilting Pattern (page 54)

Cutting
Note: *Some of the strips are listed as 20" long (for example, $2^{1}/_{2}$" x 20"). You do not need to cut them exactly 20" long. Cut a $2^{1}/_{2}$"-wide strip along the entire width of the fabric, then cut it in half. Fabrics vary in width, so the length of your strips can vary from 20" to as much as $22^{1}/_{2}$".*

Block 1
3 strips, $2^{1}/_{2}$"-wide, rust print 1
3 strips, $2^{1}/_{2}$"-wide, rust print 2
1 strip, $2^{1}/_{2}$"-wide, rust print 2 (cut in half; use one)
9 strips, $2^{1}/_{2}$"-wide, white/gold print
1 strip, $2^{1}/_{2}$"-wide, white/gold print (cut in half)
3 strips, $2^{1}/_{2}$"-wide, black
1 strip, $4^{1}/_{2}$"-wide, black (cut in half)
1 strip, $6^{1}/_{2}$"-wide, black

Block 2

3 strips, 2$\frac{1}{2}$"-wide, gold print
3 strips, 2$\frac{1}{2}$"-wide, black/rust print
1 strip, 2$\frac{1}{2}$"-wide, black/rust print (cut in half; use one)
9 strips, 2$\frac{1}{2}$"-wide, white/gold print
1 strip, 2$\frac{1}{2}$"-wide, white/gold print (cut in half)
3 strips, 2$\frac{1}{2}$"-wide, black
1 strip, 4$\frac{1}{2}$"-wide, black (cut in half)
1 strip, 6$\frac{1}{2}$"-wide, black

Block 3

3 strips, 2$\frac{1}{2}$" x 20", rust print 1
3 strips, 2$\frac{1}{2}$" x 20", black/rust print
1 strip, 2$\frac{1}{2}$" x 20", black/rust print (cut in half; use one)
9 strips, 2$\frac{1}{2}$" x 20", white/gold print
1 strip, 2$\frac{1}{2}$" x 20", white/gold print (cut in half)
3 strips, 2$\frac{1}{2}$" x 20", black
1 strip, 4$\frac{1}{2}$" x 20", black (cut in half)
1 strip, 6$\frac{1}{2}$" x 20", black

Block 4

3 strips, 2$\frac{1}{2}$" x 20", gold print
3 strips, 2$\frac{1}{2}$" x 20", rust print 2
1 strip, 2$\frac{1}{2}$" x 20", rust print 2 (cut in half; use one)
9 strips, 2$\frac{1}{2}$" x 20", white/gold print
1 strip, 2$\frac{1}{2}$" x 20", white/gold print (cut in half)
3 strips, 2$\frac{1}{2}$" x 20", black
1 strip, 4$\frac{1}{2}$" x 20", black (cut in half)
1 strip, 6$\frac{1}{2}$" x 20", black

Block 5

4 strips, 2$\frac{1}{2}$"-wide, white/gold print
2 strips, 10$\frac{1}{2}$"-wide, black
10 strips, 2$\frac{1}{2}$"-wide, black
5 strips, 10$\frac{1}{2}$"-wide, black/rust print

Finishing

10 strips, 2$\frac{1}{2}$"-wide, white/gold print (first border)
11 strips, 6$\frac{1}{2}$"-wide, black/rust print (second border)
11 strips, 2$\frac{1}{2}$"-wide, black (binding)

Instructions

Block 1

1. For rows 1 and 7, sew together a 2$\frac{1}{2}$"-wide rust print 1 strip, a 2$\frac{1}{2}$"-wide white/gold print strip, a 6$\frac{1}{2}$"-wide black strip, a 2$\frac{1}{2}$"-wide white/gold strip and a 2$\frac{1}{2}$"-wide rust print 2 strip. Press seams to one side. (**Diagram 1**)

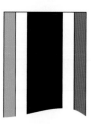

Diagram 1

2. Cut strip set at 2$\frac{1}{2}$" intervals. (**Diagram 2**) You will need twelve strips.

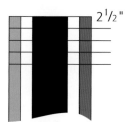

Diagram 2

3. For rows 2 and 6, sew together a 2$\frac{1}{2}$"-wide white/gold strip, a 2$\frac{1}{2}$"-wide rust print 1 strip, a 2$\frac{1}{2}$"-wide white/gold print strip, a 2$\frac{1}{2}$"-wide black strip, a 2$\frac{1}{2}$"-wide white/gold print strip, a 2$\frac{1}{2}$"-wide rust print 2 strip and a 2$\frac{1}{2}$"-wide white/gold print strip. (**Diagram 3**) Press seams to opposite direction of step 1.

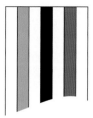

Diagram 3

4. Cut strip set at 2$\frac{1}{2}$" intervals. (**Diagram 4**) You will need twelve strips.

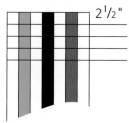

Diagram 4

5. For rows 3 and 5, sew together a 2¹/2"-wide black strip, a 2¹/2"-wide white/gold strip, a 2¹/2"-wide rust print 1 strip, a 2¹/2"-wide white/gold print strip, a 2¹/2"-wide rust print 2 strip, a 2¹/2"-wide white/gold print strip and a 2¹/2"-wide black strip. (**Diagram 5**) Press seams to opposite direction of step 3.

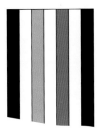

Diagram 5

6. Cut strip set at 2¹/2" intervals. (**Diagram 6**) You will need twelve strips.

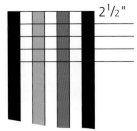

Diagram 6

7. For row 4, sew together a 4¹/2" x 20" black strip, 2¹/2" x 20" white/gold strip, a 2¹/2" x 20" rust print 2 strip, a 2¹/2" x 20" white/gold print strip and a 4¹/2" x 20" black strip. (**Diagram 7**) Press seams to opposite direction of step 5.

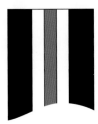

Diagram 7

8. Cut strip set at 2¹/2" intervals. (**Diagram 8**) You will need six strips.

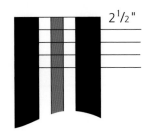

Diagram 8

9. Sew rows 1 through 7 together to complete Block 1. (**Diagram 9**) Note that rows 5, 6 and 7 are rotated before sewing. Make six Block 1.

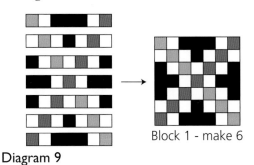

Block 1 - make 6

Diagram 9

Block 2

1. For rows 1 and 7, sew together a 2¹/2"-wide gold print strip, a 2¹/2"-wide white/gold print strip, a 6¹/2"-wide black strip, a 2¹/2"-wide white/gold strip and a 2¹/2"-wide black/rust print strip. Press seams to one side. (**Diagram 10**)

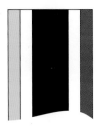

Diagram 10

2. Cut strip set at 2¹/2" intervals. (**Diagram 11**) You will need twelve strips.

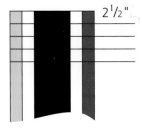

Diagram 11

47

3. For rows 2 and 6, sew together a 2^1/$_2$"-wide white/gold strip, a 2^1/$_2$"-wide gold print strip, a 2^1/$_2$"-wide white/gold print strip, a 2^1/$_2$"-wide black strip, a 2^1/$_2$"-wide white/gold print strip, a 2^1/$_2$"-wide black/rust print strip and a 2^1/$_2$"-wide white/gold print strip. (**Diagram 12**) Press seams to opposite side.

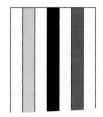

Diagram 12

4. Cut strip set at 2^1/$_2$" intervals. (**Diagram 13**) You will need twelve strips.

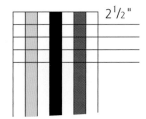

2^1/$_2$"

Diagram 13

5. For rows 3 and 5, sew together a 2^1/$_2$"-wide black strip, a 2^1/$_2$"-wide white/gold print strip, a 2^1/$_2$"-wide gold print strip, a 2^1/$_2$"-wide white/gold print strip, a 2^1/$_2$"-wide black/rust print strip, a 2^1/$_2$"-wide white/gold print strip and a 2^1/$_2$"-wide black strip. (**Diagram 14**) Press seams to one side.

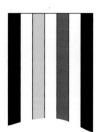

Diagram 14

6. Cut strip set at 2^1/$_2$" intervals. (**Diagram 15**) You will need twelve strips.

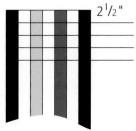

2^1/$_2$"

48   Diagram 15

7. For row 4, sew together a 4^1/$_2$" x 20" black strip, a 2^1/$_2$" x 20" white/gold print strip, 2^1/$_2$" x 20" black/rust print strip, a 2^1/$_2$" x 20" white/gold print strip and a 4^1/$_2$" x 20" black strip. (**Diagram 16**) Press seams to one side.

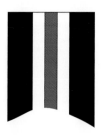

Diagram 16

8. Cut strip set at 2^1/$_2$" intervals. (**Diagram 17**) You will need six strips.

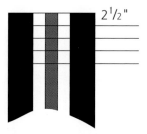

2^1/$_2$"

Diagram 17

9. Sew rows 1 through 7 together to complete Block 2. (**Diagram 18**) Note that rows 5, 6 and 7 are rotated before sewing. Make six Block 2.

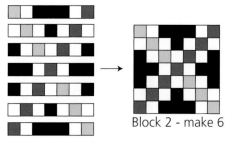

Block 2 - make 6

Diagram 18

Block 3

1. For rows 1 and 7, sew together a 2^1/$_2$"-wide rust print 1 strip, a 2^1/$_2$"-wide white/gold print strip, a 6^1/$_2$"-wide black strip, a 2^1/$_2$"-wide white/gold print strip and a 2^1/$_2$"-wide black/rust print strip. Press seams to one side. (**Diagram 19**)

Diagram 19

2. Cut strip set at $2^1/2$" intervals. (**Diagram 20**) You will need six strips.

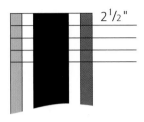

Diagram 20

3. For rows 2 and 6, sew together a $2^1/2$"-wide white/gold print strip, a $2^1/2$"-wide rust print 1 strip, a $2^1/2$"-wide white/gold print strip, a $2^1/2$"-wide black strip, a $2^1/2$"-wide white/gold print strip, a $2^1/2$"-wide black/rust print strip and a $2^1/2$"-wide white/gold print strip. (**Diagram 21**) Press seams to opposite side.

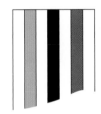

Diagram 21

4. Cut strip set at $2^1/2$" intervals. (**Diagram 22**) You will need six strips.

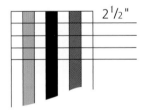

Diagram 22

5. For rows 3 and 5, sew together a $2^1/2$"-wide black strip, a $2^1/2$"-wide white/gold print strip, a $2^1/2$"-wide rust print 1 strip, a $2^1/2$"-wide, a $2^1/2$"-wide white/gold print strip, a $2^1/2$"-wide black/rust strip, a $2^1/2$"-wide white/gold print strip and a $2^1/2$"-wide black strip. (**Diagram 23**) Press seams to one side.

Diagram 23

6. Cut strip set at $2^1/2$" intervals. (**Diagram 24**) You will need six strips.

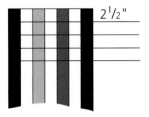

Diagram 24

7. For row 4, sew together a $4^1/2$" x 20" black strip, a $2^1/2$" x 20" white/gold print strip, a $2^1/2$" x 20" black/rust print, $2^1/2$" x 20" white/gold print and a $4^1/2$" x 20" black strip. (**Diagram 25**) Press seams to one side.

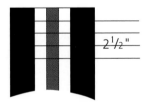

Diagram 25

8. Cut strip set at $2^1/2$" intervals. (**Diagram 26**) You will need three strips.

Diagram 26

9. Sew rows 1 through 7 together to complete Block 3. (**Diagram 27**) Note that rows 5, 6 and 7 are rotated before sewing. Make three Block 3.

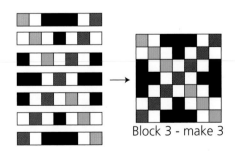

Block 3 - make 3

Diagram 27

Block 4

1. For rows 1 and 7, sew together a $2^1/2$"-wide gold print strip, a $2^1/2$"-wide white/gold print strip, a $6^1/2$"-wide black strip, a $2^1/2$"-wide white/gold print strip and a $2^1/2$"-wide rust print 2 strip. Press seams to one side. (**Diagram 28**)

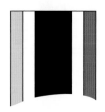

Diagram 28

2. Cut strip set at $2^1/2$" intervals. (**Diagram 29**) You will need six strips.

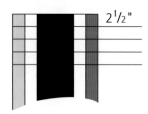

Diagram 29

3. For rows 2 and 6, sew together a $2^1/2$"-wide white/gold print strip, a $2^1/2$"-wide gold print strip, a $2^1/2$"-wide white/gold print strip, a $2^1/2$"-wide black strip, a $2^1/2$"-wide white/gold print strip, a $2^1/2$"-wide rust print 2 strip and a $2^1/2$"-wide white/gold print strip. (**Diagram 30**) Press seams to opposite side.

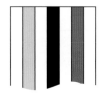

Diagram 30

4. Cut strip set at $2^1/2$" intervals. (**Diagram 31**) You will need six strips.

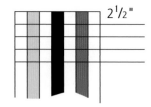

Diagram 31

5. For rows 3 and 5, sew together a $2^1/2$"-wide black strip, a $2^1/2$"-wide white/gold print strip, a $2^1/2$"-wide gold strip, a $2^1/2$"-wide, white/gold print strip, a $2^1/2$"-wide rust print 2 strip, a $2^1/2$"-wide white/gold print strip and a $2^1/2$"-wide black strip. (**Diagram 32**) Press seams to one side.

Diagram 32

6. Cut strip set at $2^1/2$" intervals. (**Diagram 33**) You will need six strips.

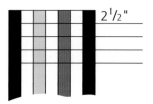

Diagram 33

7. For row 4, sew together a $4^1/2$" x 20" black strip, a $2^1/2$" x 20" white/gold print strip, a $2^1/2$" x 20" rust print 2 strip, a $2^1/2$" x 20" white/gold print and a $4^1/2$" x 20" black strip. (**Diagram 34**) Press seams to one side.

Diagram 34

8. Cut strip set at $2^1/2$" intervals. (**Diagram 35**) You will need three strips.

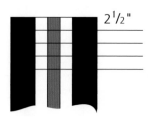

Diagram 35

50

9. Sew rows 1 through 7 together to complete Block 4. (**Diagram 36**) Note that rows 5, 6 and 7 are rotated before sewing. Make three Block 4.

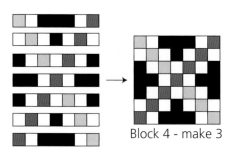

Block 4 - make 3

Diagram 36

Block 5

1. For rows 1 and 3, sew together a $2^1/2$"-wide white/gold print strip to each side of a $10^1/2$"-wide black strip. (**Diagram 37**) Press strips to one side.

Diagram 37

2. Cut strip set at $2^1/2$" intervals. (**Diagram 38**) You will need 34 strips.

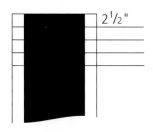

$2^1/2$"

Diagram 38

3. For row 2, sew together a $2^1/2$"-wide black strip to each side of a $10^1/2$"-wide black/rust print strip. (**Diagram 39**) Press seams to opposite side.

Diagram 39

4. Cut strip set at $10^1/2$"-wide intervals. (**Diagram 40**) You will need 17 strips.

$10^1/2$"

Diagram 40

5. Sew rows 1, 2 and 3 together to complete Block 5. (**Diagram 41**) You will need 17 Block 5.

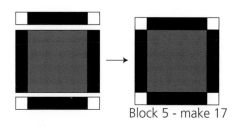

Block 5 - make 17

Diagram 41

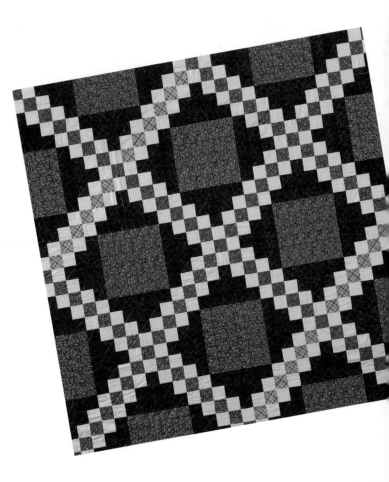

Finishing

1. Place blocks in seven rows of five blocks. (**Diagram 42**)

Block 1	Block 5	Block 2	Block 5	Block 1
Block 5	Block 3	Block 5	Block 4	Block 5
Block 2	Block 5	Block 1	Block 5	Block 2
Block 5	Block 4	Block 5	Block 3	Block 5
Block 1	Block 5	Block 2	Block 5	Block 1
Block 5	Block 3	Block 5	Block 4	Block 5
Block 2	Block 5	Block 1	Block 5	Block 2

Diagram 42

2. Sew rows together in rows, then sew rows together. Press quilt top.

3. Measure quilt lengthwise. Sew and cut two 2¹/₂"-wide white/gold strips to that length. Sew to sides of quilt. Measure quilt crosswise. Sew and cut two 2¹/₂"-wide white/gold strips to that length. Sew to top and bottom of quilt.

4. Repeat step 3 for the second border using the 6¹/₂"-wide black/rust print strips.

5. Layer and baste quilt referring to page 156.

6. Quilt diagonally through Blocks 1, 2, 3 and 4. (**Diagram 43**)

Diagram 43

7. For quilting in the plain Block 5 refer to Freezer Paper Quilting Patterns, page 19, and trace large and small quilting patterns from page 54 onto dull side of freezer paper. You will need at least 5 or 6. Cut out patterns along drawn lines.

8. Iron the small freezer paper pattern centered on top of a Block 5. Quilt next to edge of freezer paper pattern using free-form machine quilting (see page 156). Fuse a pattern onto next Block 5 and quilt next to freezer paper pattern. Once you have quilted the large design, remove paper and fuse the small pattern in the center of the block. Quilt and quilt next to the freezer paper pattern. Continue fusing and quilting until all blocks are quilted. (**Diagram 44**)

Diagram 44

9. Quilt in the ditch along seams between borders.

10. Refer to Attaching the Continuous Machine Binding, pages 157 to 158, to complete your quilt.

Irish Chain Revisited **Quilt Layout**

Flower Quilting Pattern
Enlarge pattern 162% so that it fits the block.

Pattern Note: *Trace and cut out the small and large patterns separately.*

Block 5 Quilting Detail

Mini Quilt Greeting Cards

If you can't think of a gift to give to that special person on that special occasion, these mini quilts are the answer. Using freezer paper to stabilize the fabric makes it easy to write your message on the back of the quilt.

Freezer Paper Technique
Writing on Fabric (page 17)

Approximate Size
5" x 7" each

Materials for Each Greeting Card
Fat quarter of white or light-colored fabric (backing)
Fat quarter piece background fabric
Assorted scraps
$^1/_8$ yard binding
5" x 7" batting
Freezer paper
Permanent fabric marking pens
Paper-backed fusible web
Clear monofilament thread

Patterns
Single Rose (page 59)
Angel (page 60)
Birthday Cake (page 61)
Scenic Sunset (page 62)
Christmas Tree (page 63)
Flower Bouquet (page 64)
Anniversary Bells (page 65)
Christmas Bells (page 65)

Cutting for Each Greeting Card
1 Rectangle, 5" x 7", white (backing)
1 Rectangle, 5" x 7", background (quilt top)
1 Rectangle, 5" x 7", batting
1 strip, $2^1/_2$"-wide, binding

Instructions

1. Trace pattern pieces onto paper side of paper-backed fusible web keeping pieces of the same color together. (**Diagram 1**)

Diagram 1

2. Rough cut pieces, then fuse onto wrong side of desired fabric. (**Diagram 2**)

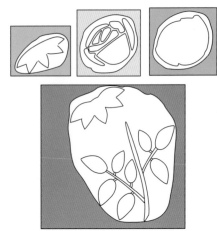

Diagram 2

3. Cut out fabric pieces along drawn lines.

4. Position pieces onto right side of background rectangle. (**Diagram 3**) When you are pleased with your arrangement, fuse carefully in place. Don't worry if your pieces are not in the exact same position as the photographed cards. Machine zigzag along raw edges of shapes using clear monofilament thread, if desired.

Diagram 3

5. Press backing rectangle onto shiny side of a 5" x 7" piece of freezer paper. Write message onto fabric. (**Diagram 4**)

Diagram 4

Note: *If you would rather print out your message, fuse an 8¹/₂" x 11" sheet of freezer paper onto your backing fabric. Type your message on your computer, then print it out onto the fabric backed with freezer paper. Remove freezer paper and cut out the message so that it is 5" x 7".*

6. Place backing with the message face down; place batting on top, then picture block on top. Quilt if desired.

7. Refer to Attaching the Continuous Machine Binding, pages 157 to 158, to complete your *Mini Quilt Greeting Card.*

Single Rose

Angel

Birthday Cake

Scenic Sunset

Christmas Tree

Flower Bouquet

Anniversary Bells

Christmas Bells

66

Take-Along Ohio Star

Because these squares can be hand pieced, this is a project that you can take with you and whip out whenever you have a few minutes to stitch. Freezer paper templates will make your hand piecing easier and quicker than tracing templates onto your fabric.

Freezer Paper Technique
Hand Piecing (pages 17 to 19)

Approximate Size
28" x 28"

Block Size
9" x 9" finished

Materials
$^1/_4$ yard red print
$^1/_4$ yard gold print
$^1/_4$ yard light blue print
$^1/_4$ yard dark blue print
$^5/_8$ yard medium blue print (border and binding)
1 yard backing
Batting
Freezer paper
Removable fabric pen or pencil (optional)

Patterns
A Diamond (page 71)
A reversed Diamond (page 71)
B Triangle (page 71)
C Square (page 71)

Cutting
Blocks

Note: *Trace 16 of each pattern onto dull side of freezer paper. Fuse the freezer paper patterns onto wrong side of fabric according to the cutting instructions. Cut fabric $^1/_4$" from edge of freezer paper. Do not remove freezer paper patterns. (Diagram 1)*

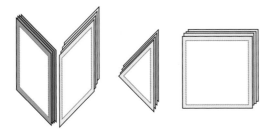

Diagram 1

16 A Diamonds, red print
16 A reversed Diamonds, gold print
16 B Triangles, light blue print
16 C Squares, light blue print

Finishing

2 strips, $2^{1}/2"$ x $9^{1}/2"$, dark blue print (sashing)
3 strips, $2^{1}/2"$ x $20^{1}/2"$, dark blue print (sashing)
2 strips, $2^{1}/2"$ x $24^{1}/2"$, dark blue print (sashing)
2 strips, $2^{1}/2"$ x $24^{1}/2"$, medium blue print (border)
2 strips, $2^{1}/2"$ x $28^{1}/2"$, medium blue print (border)
2 strips, $2^{1}/2"$-wide, medium blue print (binding)

Instructions

Ohio Star Blocks

1. Place a red print A Diamond right sides together with a gold print A reversed Diamond. Stitch pieces together along freezer paper edge, knotting thread at the beginning and end of stitching. **Note:** *Stitch along freezer paper edge only, not end to end.* (**Diagram 2**)

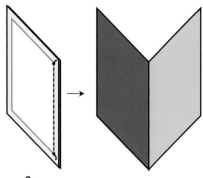

Diagram 2

2. Place a short edge of a light blue print B Triangle right sides together with the red print A Diamond. Sew along freezer paper edge. (**Diagram 3**)

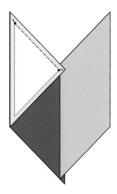

Diagram 3

3. Carefully place adjacent short edge of light blue print B Triangle right sides together with gold print A reversed Diamond. Sew in place along freezer paper edge. (**Diagram 4**)

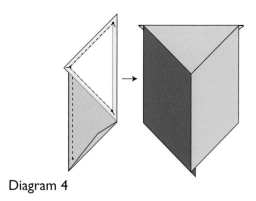

Diagram 4

4. Repeat steps 2 to 4 for three more A/A reversed/B units.

5. Sew two A/A reversed/B units together along short freezer paper edge of Diamonds. (**Diagram 5**) Repeat.

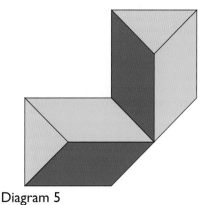

Diagram 5

6. Sew units from step 5 together (**Diagram 6**)

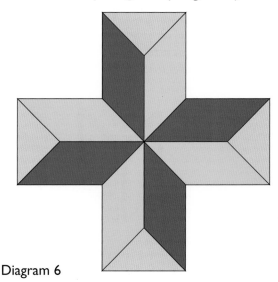

Diagram 6

7. Sew a light blue C Square in corner of Star. Sew along one edge of freezer paper square, sewing from inner corner to outer edge. Repeat along adjacent edge of Square. Repeat at remaining three corners to complete Ohio Star block. (**Diagram 7**)

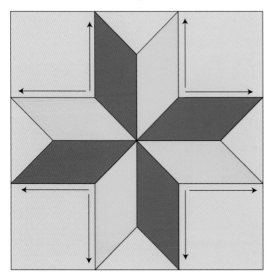

Diagram 7

8. Repeat steps 1 to 7 for three more Ohio Star blocks.

Finishing

Note: *If hand piecing sashing and borders to quilt top, draw a line ¹/₄" from each edge of right side of each sashing and border strip using a regular lead pencil.*

1. Sew a 2¹/₂" x 9¹/₂" dark blue print strip in between two Ohio Star blocks; repeat. Sew rows to 2¹/₂" x 20¹/₂" dark blue print strip. (**Diagram 8**)

Diagram 8

2. Sew a 2¹/₂" x 20¹/₂" dark blue print strip to each side of quilt top. Sew 2¹/₂" x 24¹/₂" dark blue print strips to top and bottom of quilt top. (**Diagram 9**)

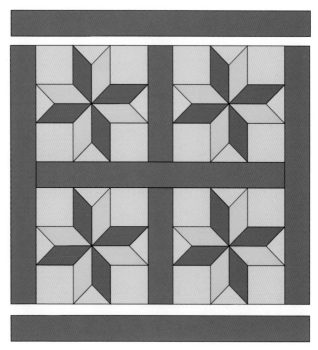

Diagram 9

3. Sew a 2¹/₂" x 24¹/₂" medium blue print strip to each side of quilt top. Sew a 2¹/₂" x 28¹/₂" medium blue print strip to top and bottom of quilt top.

4. Refer to Finishing Your Quilt, pages 156 to 159, to complete your quilt.

Take-along Ohio Stars **Quilt Layout**

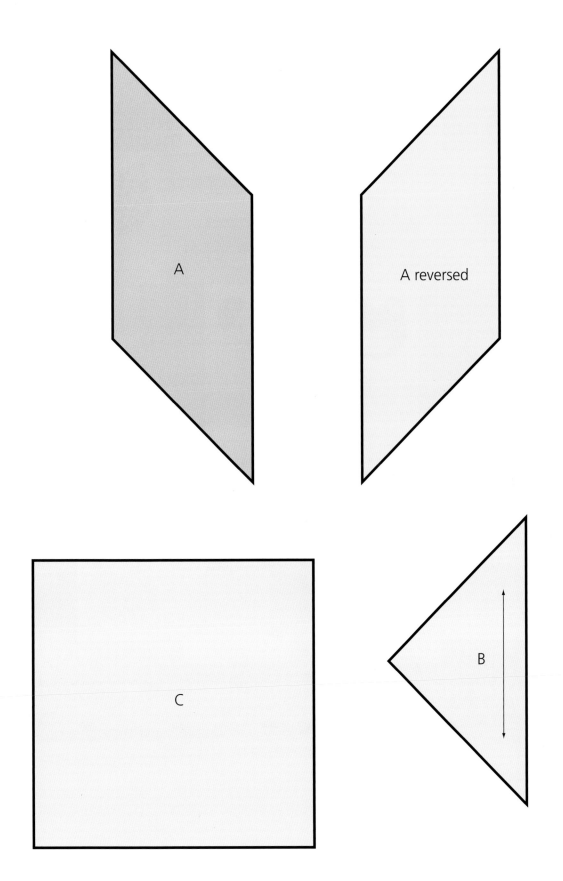

Log Cabin Zoo

What child wouldn't love this quilt filled with his favorite animals. First you use freezer paper to make the foundation-pieced Log Cabin blocks; then, you use freezer paper to make the appliquéd animal blocks which sit in the center of some of the Log Cabins. Finally you get hugs and kisses from a grateful child.

Freezer Paper Techniques
Foundation Piecing (pages 7 to 14)
Appliqué with Fusible Interfacing (pages 14 to 17)

Approximate Size
41" x 41"

Block Size
8" x 8" finished

Materials
$^{1}/_{3}$ yard very light green fabric
$^{1}/_{4}$ yard light green fabric
$^{1}/_{4}$ yard medium green fabric
$^{1}/_{3}$ yard dark green fabric (includes first border and cornerstones)
$1^{1}/_{4}$ yard animal novelty print (includes blocks centers, second border, and binding)
$^{1}/_{4}$ yard cream fabric
1 to 2 yards backing (**Note:** *The yardage amount depends on width of backing fabric used.*)
Batting
Freezer paper
Permanent black fabric marker
Paper-backed fusible web
Clear monofilament thread

Patterns
Log Cabin A (page 77)
Log Cabin B (page 78)
Bear (page 79)
Dog (page 79)
Rabbit (page 79)
Cat (page 80)
Monkey (page 80)
Lion (page 81)
Duck (page 81)
Elephant (page 81)

Cutting

Note: *Refer to Foundation Piecing Methods 1 and 2 for cutting pieces. You will need the following pieces.*

Log Cabin A

8 squares, 3" x 3", animal novelty print (1)
8 strips, $1^7/8$" x 3", light green (2)
8 strips, $1^7/8$" x $4^3/8$", very light green (3)
8 strips, $1^7/8$" x $4^3/8$", medium green (4)
8 strips, $1^7/8$" x $5^3/4$", medium green (5)
8 strips, $1^7/8$" x $5^3/4$", light green (6)
8 strips, $1^7/8$" x $7^1/8$", very light green (7)
8 strips, $1^7/8$" x $7^1/8$", medium green (8)
8 strips, $1^7/8$" x $8^1/2$", dark green (9)

Log Cabin B

8 squares, $5^3/4$" x $5^3/4$", cream (1)
8 strips, $1^7/8$" x $5^3/4$", light green (2)
8 strips, $1^7/8$" x $7^1/8$", very light green (3)
8 strips, $1^7/8$" x $7^1/8$", medium green (4)
8 strips, $1^7/8$" x $8^1/2$", dark green (5)

Finishing

4 strips, 2"-wide, dark green (first border)
4 strips, $3^1/2$"-wide, animal novelty print (second border)
4 squares, $3^1/2$" x $3^1/2$", dark green (cornerstones)
4 strips, $2^1/2$"-wide, animal novelty print (binding)

Instructions

Block A

1. Make eight Log Cabin block A using Foundation Piecing Method 1 or 2, pages 7 to 14. (**Diagram 1**)

make 8

Diagram 1

Log Cabin B

1. Make 8 Log Cabin block B using Foundation Piecing Method 1 or 2. (**Diagram 2**)

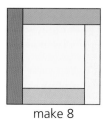

make 8

Diagram 2

2. Refer to Easy Appliqué, page 16, and individual pattern notes, pages 79 to 81, to prepare animal features with paper-backed fusible web.

3. Referring to Appliqué with Fusible Interfacing, pages 16 to 17 and **Diagram 3**, appliqué animals to centers of blocks noting positions of Log Cabin blocks. Placement of animals is very important if you want your quilt to look like the photographed quilt. Fuse animal features such as ears, noses, muzzles, etc. to animals referring to individual patterns. Draw remaining features on animals using a black permanent fabric marker.

Diagram 3

4. Using clear monofilament thread and a small machine zigzag, sew along raw edges of fused facial features.

Finishing

1. Place blocks in four rows of four blocks. Sew blocks together in rows. Press seams for rows in alternating directions; sew rows together. (**Diagram 4**)

Diagram 4

2. Measure quilt lengthwise. Cut two 2"-wide dark green strips to that length. Sew to sides of quilt. Measure quilt crosswise. Cut two 2"-wide dark green strips to that length. Sew to top and bottom of quilt.

3. Measure quilt lengthwise and crosswise. Cut four $3^1/2$" x $3^1/2$" animal novelty print strips to that length. Sew strips to sides of quilt. Press strips toward border. Sew a $3^1/2$" x $3^1/2$" dark green square to each end of remaining $3^1/2$" animal novelty print strips; press seams toward border strip. Sew to top and bottom of quilt. Press seams toward border.

4. Refer to Finishing Your Quilt, pages 156 to 159, to complete your quilt.

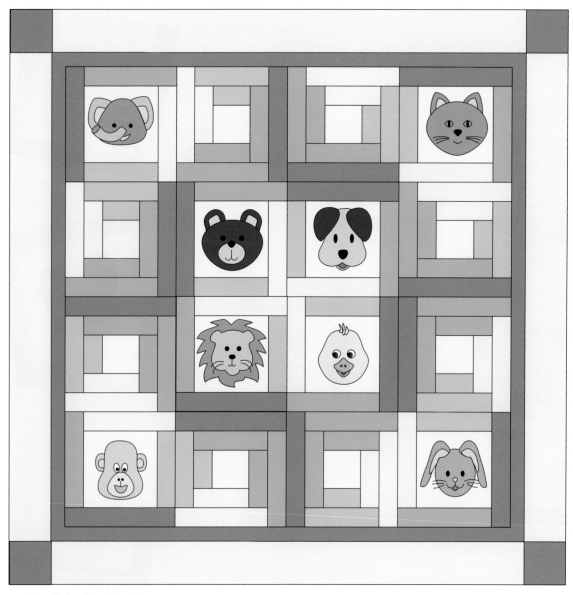

Log Cabin Zoo **Quilt Layout**

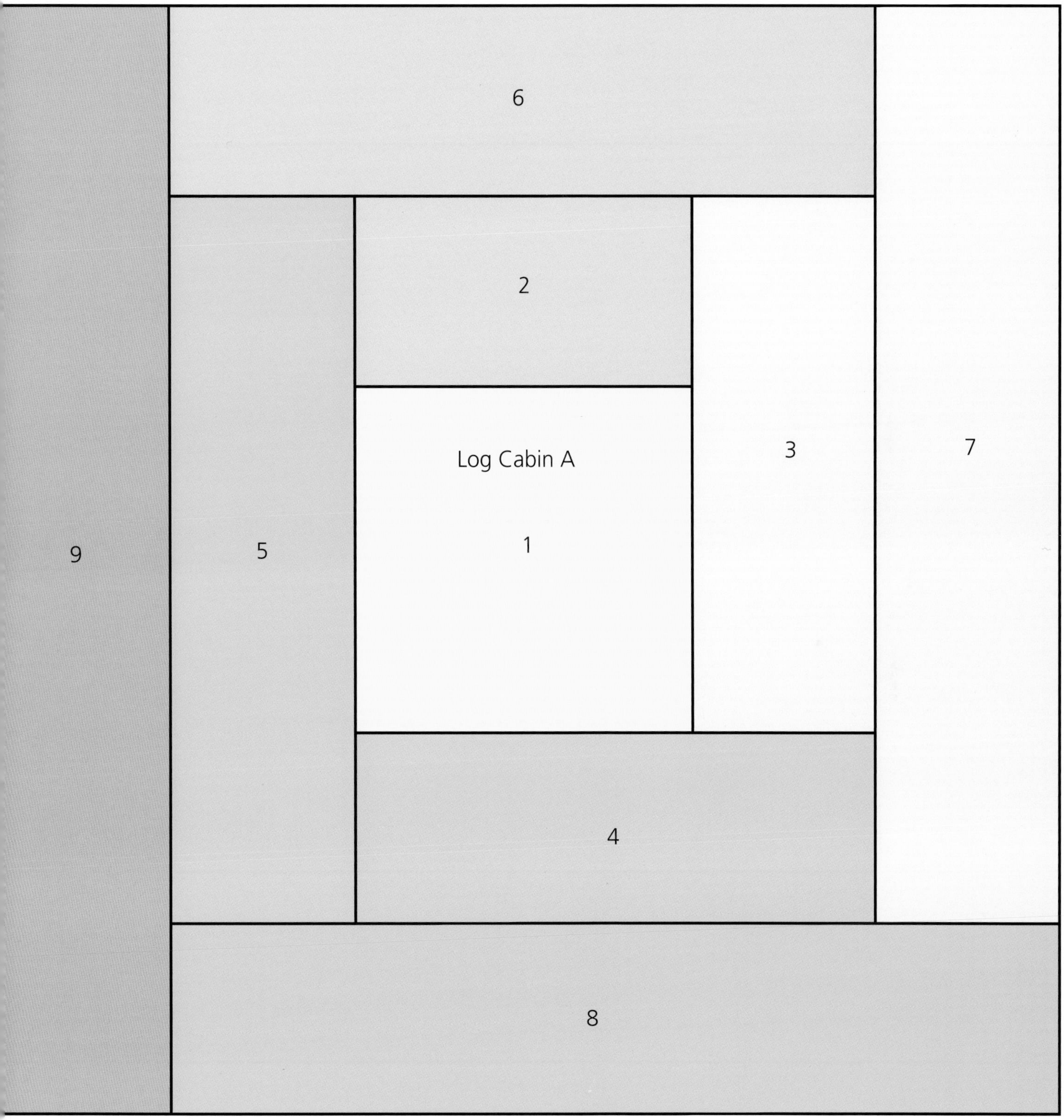

6

2

3

7

Log Cabin A

5

1

9

4

8

3

2

Log Cabin B

1

4

5

Bear Pattern Notes: *Trace entire outline (head and ears) of Bear onto dull side of freezer paper and refer to Appliqué with Fusible Interfacing, pages 16 to 17 to appliqué Bear in center of Log Cabin B. Trace pink ears and tan muzzle onto paper side of fusible web referring to Easy Appliqué, page 16. Fuse in place on Bear. Draw eyes, nose and mouth with permanent black fabric marker.*

Rabbit Pattern Notes: *Trace entire outline (head and ears) of Rabbit onto dull side of freezer paper and refer to Appliqué with Fusible Interfacing, pages 16 to 17 to appliqué Rabbit in center of Log Cabin B. Trace, pink inner ears, pink nose and pink tongue onto paper side of fusible web referring to Easy Appliqué, page 16. Fuse in place on Rabbit. Draw eyes, whiskers, and mouth with permanent black fabric marker.*

Dog Pattern Notes: *Trace entire outline (head and mouth) of Dog onto dull side of freezer paper and refer to Appliqué with Fusible Interfacing, pages 16 to 17 to appliqué Dog in center of Log Cabin B. Trace dark brown ears, pink tongue and black nose onto paper side of fusible web referring to Easy Appliqué, page 16. Fuse in place on Dog. Draw eyes with permanent black fabric marker.*

Cat Pattern Notes: *Trace entire outline (head and ears) of Cat onto dull side of freezer paper and refer to Appliqué with Fusible Interfacing, pages 16 to 17 to appliqué Cat in center of Log Cabin B. Trace pink inner ears, green eyes, and black nose onto paper side of fusible web referring to Easy Appliqué, page 16. Fuse in place on Cat. Draw pupils in eyes, whiskers and mouth with permanent black fabric marker.*

Monkey Pattern Notes: *Trace entire outline (head and ears) of Monkey onto dull side of freezer paper and refer to Appliqué with Fusible Interfacing, pages 16 to 17 to appliqué Monkey in center of Log Cabin B. Trace pink inner ears, pink mouth, tan muzzle and white eyes onto paper side of fusible web referring to Easy Appliqué, page 16. Fuse in place on Monkey. Draw eyes and nose with permanent black fabric marker.*

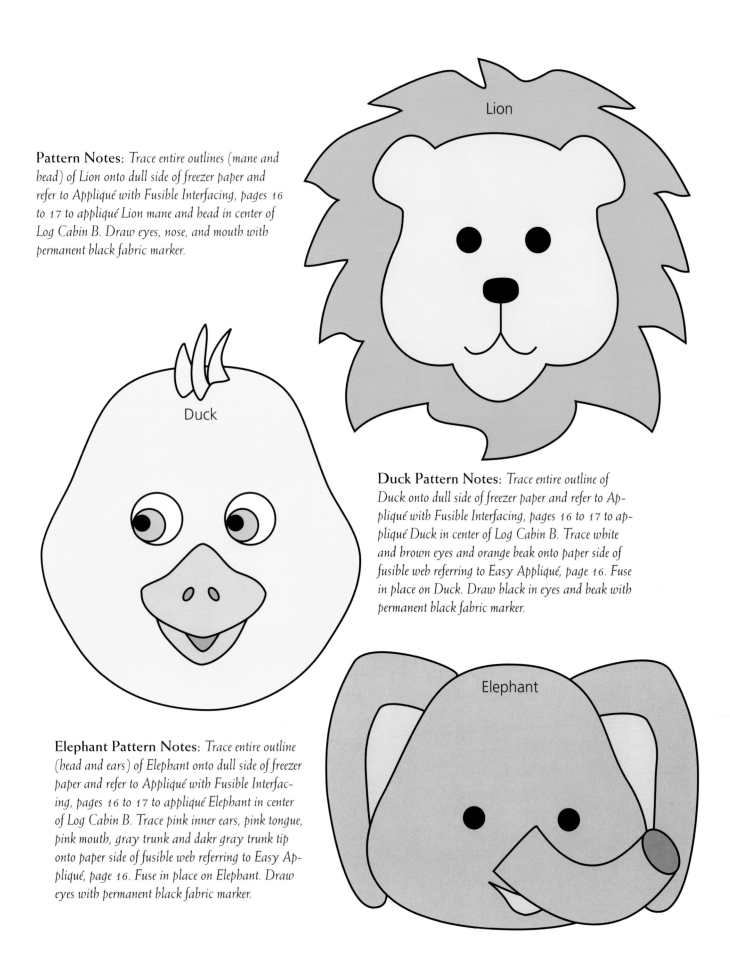

Pattern Notes: *Trace entire outlines (mane and head) of Lion onto dull side of freezer paper and refer to Appliqué with Fusible Interfacing, pages 16 to 17 to appliqué Lion mane and head in center of Log Cabin B. Draw eyes, nose, and mouth with permanent black fabric marker.*

Duck Pattern Notes: *Trace entire outline of Duck onto dull side of freezer paper and refer to Appliqué with Fusible Interfacing, pages 16 to 17 to appliqué Duck in center of Log Cabin B. Trace white and brown eyes and orange beak onto paper side of fusible web referring to Easy Appliqué, page 16. Fuse in place on Duck. Draw black in eyes and beak with permanent black fabric marker.*

Elephant Pattern Notes: *Trace entire outline (head and ears) of Elephant onto dull side of freezer paper and refer to Appliqué with Fusible Interfacing, pages 16 to 17 to appliqué Elephant in center of Log Cabin B. Trace pink inner ears, pink tongue, pink mouth, gray trunk and dakr gray trunk tip onto paper side of fusible web referring to Easy Appliqué, page 16. Fuse in place on Elephant. Draw eyes with permanent black fabric marker.*

Christmas Stars & Angels

The angels in the picture blocks come from a novelty print, but the stars are your creations, made especially quick using the foundation piecing method with freezer paper. You'll want to make several to decorate every bed in your house at Christmas.

Freezer Paper Technique
Foundation Piecing Method 1 or 2 (pages 7 to 14)

Approximate Size
$48^1/2$" x $63^1/2$"

Block Size
$7^1/2$" x $7^1/2$" finished

Materials
1 yard novelty print 1
1 yard red fabric
1 yard green fabric (includes first border)
1 yard gold fabric
1 yard red/green floral fabric (includes cornerstones)
1 yard pink fabric
1 yard light gold fabric
1 yard novelty print 2 (second border)
$^1/2$ yard dark red fabric (binding)
3 yards backing
Batting
Freezer paper

Patterns
Star Block A and B (1/4 pattern) (page 87)

Cutting

Star Blocks

Note: *Read Foundation Piecing Methods 1 and 2, pages 7 to 14. For Foundation Piecing Method 1, you do not need to cut exact pieces. For Foundation Piecing Method 2, cut pieces listed below.*
72 Shape A1, light gold
72 Shape A2, red/green floral
72 Shape A3, green
72 Shape A4, red
72 Shape B1, pink
72 Shape B2, green
72 Shape B3, red
72 Shape B4, gold

Pictures Blocks

17 Squares, 6" x 6", novelty print 1
34 strips, 1$\frac{1}{2}$" x 6", red/green floral
34 strips, 1$\frac{1}{2}$" x 8", red/green floral

Finishing

5 strips, 2"-wide, green (first border)
5 strips, 4$\frac{1}{2}$"-wide, novelty print 2 (second border)
4 squares, 4$\frac{1}{2}$" x 4$\frac{1}{2}$", red/green floral (cornerstones)
6 strips, 2$\frac{1}{2}$"-wide, dark red (binding)

Instructions

Star Blocks

1. Make 18 Star blocks referring to Foundation Piecing Method 1 or 2, pages 7 to 14. (**Diagram 1**)

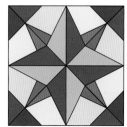

Star Block - make 18

Diagram 1

Picture Blocks

1. Sew 1$\frac{1}{2}$" x 6" red/green floral strip to opposite sides of 6" x 6" novelty print 1 square. Press seams toward strip. (**Diagram 2**)

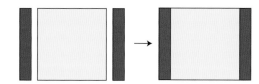

Diagram 2

2. Sew 1$\frac{1}{2}$" x 8" red/green floral strip to remaining sides of 6" x 6" novelty print 1 square to complete Picture block. (**Diagram 3**) Make 17 Picture blocks.

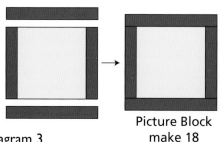

Picture Block
make 18

Diagram 3

Finishing

1. Arrange Star blocks and Picture blocks in seven rows of five blocks each. (**Diagram 4**)

Diagram 4

2. Sew blocks in rows. Press seams for rows in alternating directions. Sew rows together.

3. Measure quilt lengthwise. Sew and cut two 2"-wide green strips to that length. Sew to sides of quilt top. Measure quilt crosswise. Sew and cut two 2"-wide green strips to that length. Sew to top and bottom of quilt.

4. Measure quilt top lengthwise. Sew and cut two $4^1/2$"-wide novelty print 2 strips to that length. Measure quilt crosswise; sew and cut two $4^1/2$"-wide novelty print 2 strips to that length. (**Diagram 5**)

Diagram 5

5. Sew the lengthwise novelty print 2 strips to the sides of the quilt top. Sew $4^1/2$" x $4^1/2$" red/green floral squares to each end of crosswise novelty print 2 strips. Sew to top and bottom of quilt. (**Diagram 6**)

Diagram 6

6. Refer to Finishing Your Quilt, pages 156 to 159, to complete your quilt.

Christmas Stars & Angels **Quilt Layout**

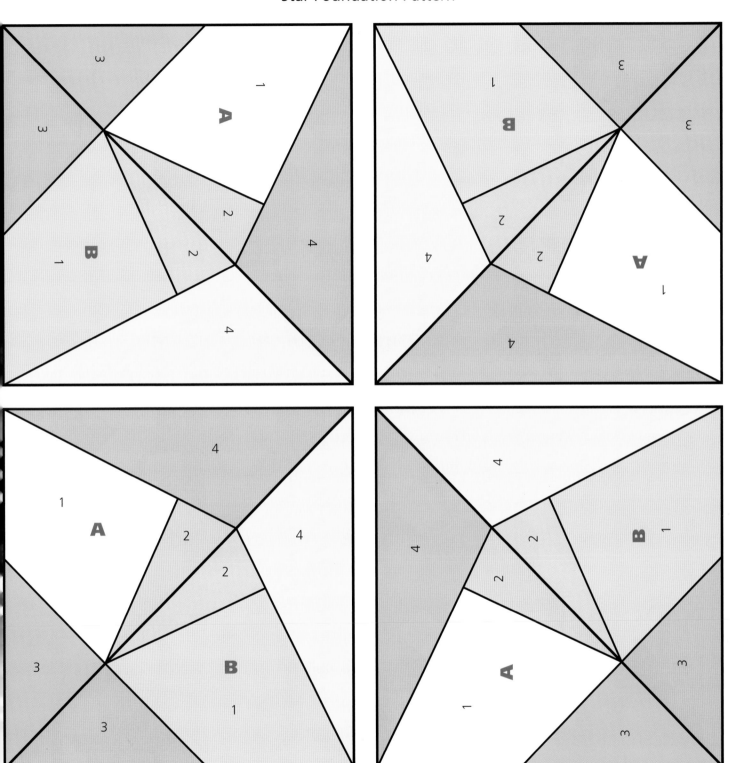

Tulips in the Garden

At first glance you may think that the only tulips in this quilt are the purple ones made with the tulip block pattern. Look closely, and you will find tulips and their leaves dancing across the quilt in the quilting patterns. Using freezer paper, these quilting patterns are created quickly.

Freezer Paper Technique
Freezer Paper Quilting Patterns (page 19)

Approximate Size
$68^1/2$" x $92^1/2$"

Block Size
12" x 12" finished

Materials
$3/4$ yard dark purple/gold fabric
1 yard light purple fabric
1 yard dark green/gold fabric
1 yard light green fabric (includes first border)
$1/2$ yard light green floral fabric
$1/2$ yard light cream floral fabric
2 yards white fabric
1 yard large floral print fabric (second border)
$3/4$ yard binding
Batting
Freezer paper

Patterns
Tulip Quilting Pattern (page 94)
Leaf Quilt Pattern (page 94)

Cuting
Blocks
48 Rectangles, 3" x 4", dark purple/gold
14 Rectangles, 3" x $6^1/2$", dark purple/gold
36 Squares, 4" x 4", light cream floral
68 Rectangles, 3" x $6^1/2$", dark green/gold
68 Rectangles, 3" x 4", light green
34 Squares, 4" x 4", light green floral
24 rectangles, 3" x 4", light purple
48 Rectangles, 3" x $6^1/2$", light purple
140 Squares, 3" x 3", white
70 Squares, 4" x 4", white

Finishing
8 strips, $1^3/4$"-wide, light green (first border)
8 strips, $3^1/2$"-wide, large floral print (second border)
8 strips, $2^1/2$"-wide, binding

Instructions

Blocks

1. For Block 1, sew a 3" x 4" dark purple/gold rectangle to a 4" x 4" light cream floral square. Press seam toward strip. (**Diagram 1**)

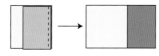

Diagram 1

2. Sew a 3" x 6½" light purple rectangle to adjacent side of the 4" x 4" light cream floral square. (**Diagram 2**) Press seam toward light purple.

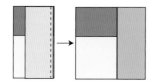

Diagram 2

3. Place a 3" x 3" white square right sides together with dark purple/gold rectangle; sew diagonally from corner to corner. Trim ¼" from stitching; press open resulting triangle. (**Diagram 3**)

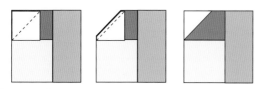

Diagram 3

Hint: *If you are unsure of sewing diagonally on a blank square, mark a diagonal line on wrong side of the squares. Sew along drawn line.*

4. Repeat step 3 on light purple rectangle with a 3" x 3" white square. (**Diagram 4**) Make 24 Unit A.

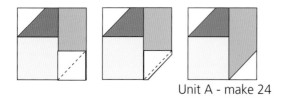

Unit A - make 24

Diagram 4

5. Repeat steps 1 to 4 using 4" x 4" white square instead of 4" x 4" light cream floral square. (**Diagram 5**). Make 24 Unit B.

Unit B - make 24

Diagram 5

6. Sew Unit A to Unit B. Repeat. (**Diagram 6**)

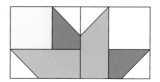

Diagram 6

7. Sew Units A/B together to complete Block 1. (**Diagram 7**) Make 12 Block 1.

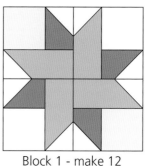

Block 1 - make 12

Diagram 7

Block 2

1. Sew a 3" x 4" light purple rectangle to a 4" x 4" light cream floral square. (**Diagram 8**) Press seam toward strip.

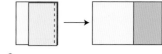

Diagram 8

2. Sew a 3" x 6½" dark purple/gold rectangle to adjacent side. (**Diagram 9**) Press seam.

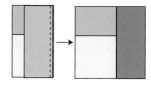

Diagram 9

3. Place a 3" x 3" white square right sides together with light purple rectangle; sew diagonally from corner to corner. (**Diagram 10**)

Diagram 10

4. Trim ¼" from stitching; press open resulting triangle. Repeat step 3 using a 3" x 3" white square on the dark purple rectangle. (**Diagram 11**) Make 12 Unit C.

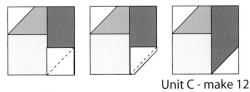

Unit C - make 12

Diagram 11

5. Repeat steps 1 to 4 using 4" x 4" white square. (**Diagram 12**) Make 12 Unit D.

Unit D - make 12

Diagram 12

6. Sew Unit C to Unit D. Repeat. (**Diagram 13**)

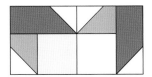

Diagram 13

7. Sew Units C/D together to complete Block 2. (**Diagram 14**) Make six Block 2.

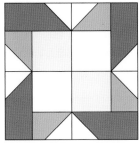

Block 2 - make 6

Diagram 14

Block 3

1. Sew a 3" x 4" light green rectangle to a 4" x 4" light green floral square. (**Diagram 15**) Press.

Diagram 15

2. Sew a 3" x 6½" dark green rectangle to adjacent side. (**Diagram 16**) Press.

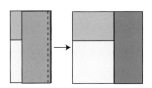

Diagram 16

3. Place a 3" x 3" white square right sides together with a dark green/gold rectangle; sew diagonally from corner to corner. (**Diagram 17**) Trim ¼" from stitching and press open resulting triangle.

Diagram 17

4. Repeat step 3 with 3" x 3" white square on the light green rectangle to complete Unit E. (**Diagram 18**) Make 34 Unit E.

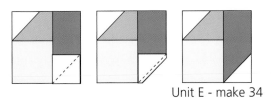

Unit E - make 34

Diagram 18

5. Repeat steps 1 to 4 using white 4" x 4" squares instead of the 4" x 4" light green floral squares. (**Diagram 19**) Make 34 Unit F.

Unit F - make 34

Diagram 19

6. Sew a Unit E and Unit F together. (**Diagram 20**) Repeat.

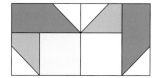

Diagram 20

7. Sew Units E/F together to complete Block 3. (**Diagram 21**)

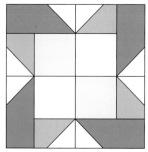

Block 3 - make 17

Diagram 21

Finishing

1. For rows 1, 3, 5, and 7, sew Blocks 1 and 3 together. (**Diagram 22**)

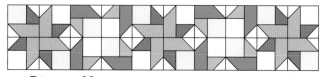

Diagram 22

2. For rows 2, 4, and 6, sew Blocks 2 and 3 together. (**Diagram 23**)

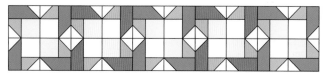

Diagram 23

3. Sew rows together. (**Diagram 24**)

Diagram 24

4. Measure quilt lengthwise. Sew and cut two $1^{3}/4$"-wide light green strips to that length. Sew to sides of quilt. Measure quilt crosswise. Sew and cut two $1^{3}/4$"-wide light green strips to that length. Sew to top and bottom of quilt.

5. Repeat step 4 for second border using $3^{1}/2$"-wide large floral strips. Press quilt top.

6. Layer and baste quilt referring to pages 156 to 157.

7. Trace Tulip and Leaf Quilting patterns from page 94 onto dull side of freezer paper. You will need at least 20 to 24 of each design since you can re-fuse freezer paper three to four times before it loses its fusibility. **Hint**: *Pin freezer paper pattern to quilt if it doesn't stick properly.*

8. Starting in center, position freezer paper patterns shiny side down on blocks to be quilted. Fuse in place.

9. Quilt next to edge of freezer paper pattern. When you are finished quilting the first row of blocks, remove from sewing machine and remove freezer paper patterns. Position freezer paper onto next row of blocks; fuse in place. Quilt around motifs. Continue quilting and re-positioning patterns until entire quilt is quilted.

10. Refer to Finishing Your Quilt, pages 156 to 159, to complete your quilt.

Tulips in the Garden **Quilt Layout**

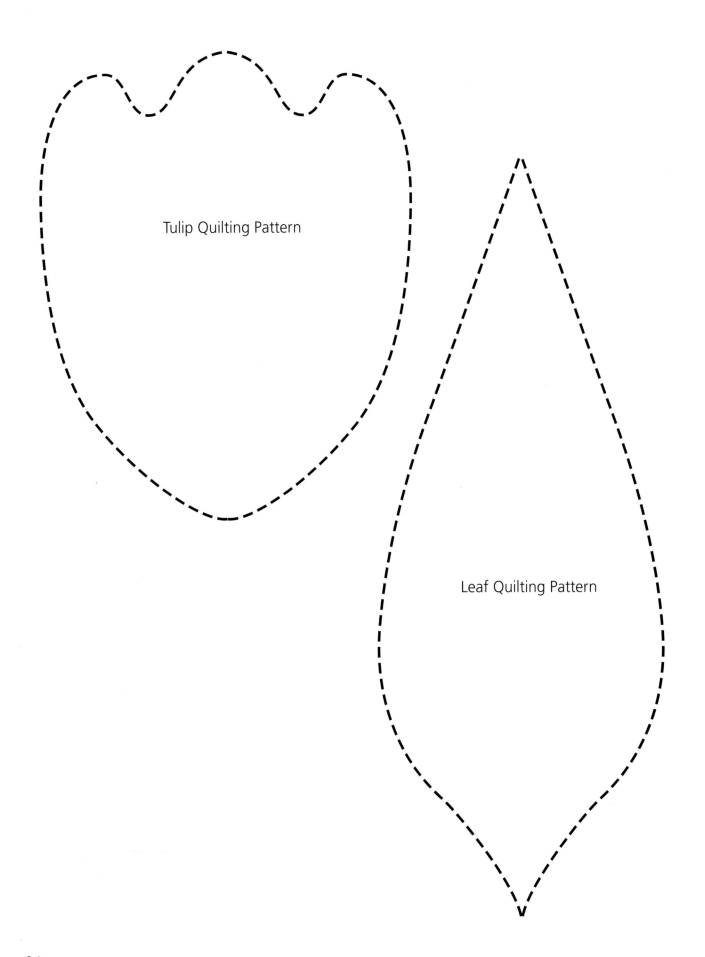

Tulip Quilting Pattern

Leaf Quilting Pattern

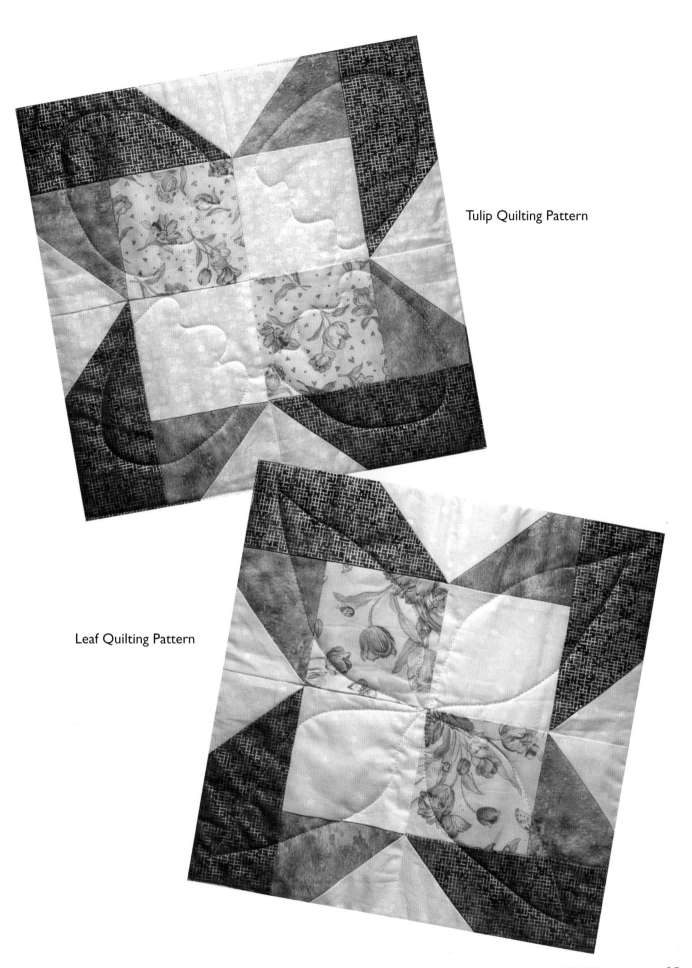

Tulip Quilting Pattern

Leaf Quilting Pattern

Quilted Memories

What do you do with the photos you take while on a trip? Put them into a quilt as I did in this quilt filled with photos taken in and around Monterey, California. By printing the photos on the fabric with freezer paper, I was able to complete the quilt while the memories were still fresh.

Freezer Paper Technique
Printing Photos on Fabric (page 6)

Approximate Size
29" x 37"

Block Size
8" x 8" finished

Materials
1 yard turquoise print
1 yard dark blue print
*$^{1}/_{2}$ yard white fabric (photos)
$^{3}/_{8}$ yard light blue fabric (first border)
$^{5}/_{8}$ yard black/gold print (second border, binding)
1 yard backing
Batting
Freezer paper
12 photos, 4" x 4" square (seam allowances will be added
   when cutting from fabric)

*Read Printing Photos on Fabric, page 6. You must treat your own fabric using Bubble Jet Set 2000 and Bubble Jet Rinse.

Cutting
Blocks
Note: *Do not cut white squares until you print the photos. Read Printing Photos on Fabric, page 6, to print photos before cutting squares. Be sure photos fit into a 4" x 4" finished square. Add $^{1}/_{4}$" to each edge to cut $4^{1}/_{2}$" x $4^{1}/_{2}$" squares.*

12 squares, $4^{1}/_{2}$" x $4^{1}/_{2}$", white (photos)
2 strips, $2^{1}/_{2}$"-wide, dark blue print
2 strips, $4^{1}/_{2}$"-wide, dark blue print
2 strips, $2^{1}/_{2}$"-wide, turquoise print
2 strips, $4^{1}/_{2}$"-wide, turquoise print

Finishing
3 strips, $1^{1}/_{2}$"-wide, light blue (first border)
3 strips, 2"-wide, black/gold print (second border)
4 strips, $2^{1}/_{2}$"-wide, black/gold print (binding)

Instructions

Preparing Photos

1. Refer to Printing Photos on Fabric, page 6, to prepare fabric and print 4" x 4" photos onto fabric. When cutting out photos, add $^1/_4$" seam allowance along each edge for a $4^1/_2$" x $4^1/_2$" square.

Note: *If you would like to put a caption on your photo, type a short description then position it along the lower edge of the photo before printing onto fabric.*

Blocks

1. Sew a $2^1/_2$"-wide dark blue print strip to a $2^1/_2$"-wide turquoise print strip. Press seams to one side. (**Diagram 1**)

Diagram 1

2. Cut strip set at $2^1/_2$" intervals. (**Diagram 2**) You will need 24 strips.

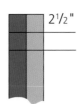

Diagram 2

3. Sew strips to opposite sides of $4^1/_2$" x $4^1/_2$" photo square, noting position. (**Diagram 3**) Press seams away from photo.

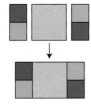

Diagram 3

4. Sew a $4^1/_2$"-wide dark blue print strip to a $4^1/_2$"-wide turquoise print strip. Press seams to one side. (**Diagram 4**)

Diagram 4

5. Cut strip set at $2^1/_2$" intervals. (**Diagram 5**) You will need 24 strips.

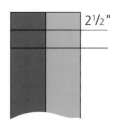

Diagram 5

6. Sew strips to remaining sides of photo, noting position, to complete block. (**Diagram 6**) Press seams away from photo.

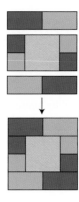

Diagram 6

7. Repeat steps 1 to 6 for 11 more blocks.

Finishing

1. Position blocks in four rows of three blocks. Sew blocks together in rows. (**Diagram 7**) Press seams for rows in opposite directions; sew rows together.

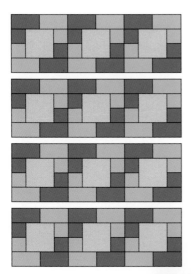

Diagram 7

2. Measure quilt lengthwise. Cut two 1^1/$_2$"-wide light blue strips to that length; sew to sides of quilt. Measure quilt crosswise. Cut two 1^1/$_2$"-wide light blue strips to that length; sew to top and bottom quilt.

3. Repeat step 2 for second border using 2^1/$_2$"-wide black/gold print strips.

4. Refer to Finishing Your Quilt, pages 156 to 159, to complete your quilt.

Quilted Memories **Quilt Layout**

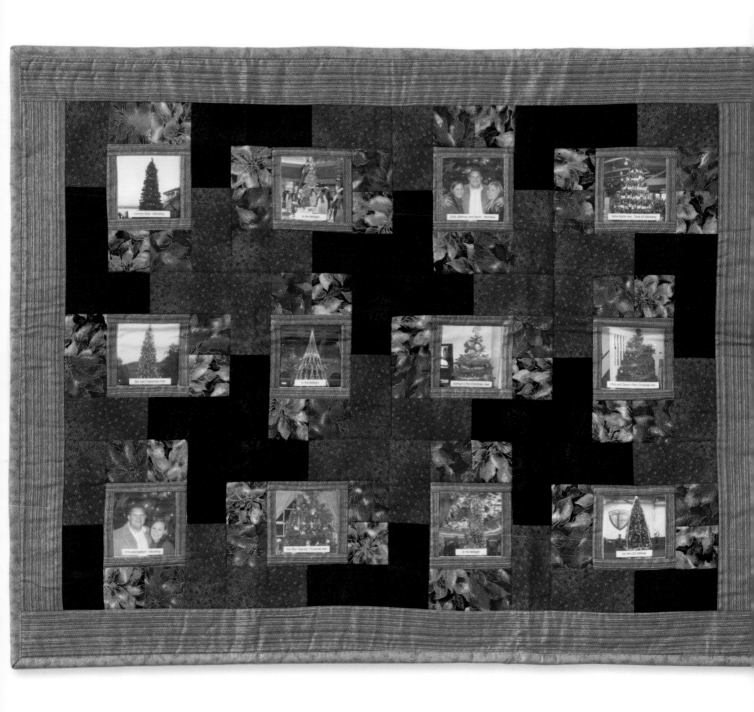

Christmas Trees

Every Christmas I see so many beautiful Christmas trees with which I'd love to decorate my house. Why not photograph those trees, transfer them on to fabric with freezer paper and make a Christmas wall hanging! So here are trees from the Bellagio in Las Vegas to San Juan Capistrano Park and, of course, from my family.

Freezer Paper Technique
Printing Photos on Fabric (page 6)

Approximate Size
36" x 28"

Block Size
8" x 8" finished

Materials
$^1/_2$ yard red print
$^1/_2$ yard green print
$^1/_2$ yard dark red fabric
$^1/_2$ yard dark green fabric
*$^1/_2$ yard white fabric (photos)
$^1/_4$ yard gold stripe (includes border)
$^3/_8$ yard gold fabric (binding)
1 yard backing
Batting
Freezer paper
12 photos, 3" x 3" square (seam allowances will be added
when cutting from fabric)

*Read Printing Photos on Fabric, page 6. You must treat your fabric using Bubble
Jet Set 2000 and Bubble Jet Rinse.*

Cutting
Blocks
*12 squares $3^1/_2$" x $3^1/_2$", white (photos)
24 strips, 1" x $3^1/_2$", gold stripe
24 strips, 1" x $4^1/_2$", gold stripe
2 strips, $2^1/_2$"-wide, red print
2 strips, $4^1/_2$"-wide, dark red fabric
2 strips, $2^1/_2$"-wide, green print
2 strips, $4^1/_2$"-wide, dark green fabric
*Do not cut white squares until you print the photos. Refer to Printing Photos on Fabric to
    prepare fabric and print photos. Be sure photos will fit into a 3" x 3" finished square,
    then add $^1/_4$" around each edge to cut out photos.

Finishing
3 strips, $2^1/_2$"-wide, gold stripe (border)
4 strips, $2^1/_2$"-wide, gold (binding)

Instructions

Preparing Photos

1. Refer to Printing Photos on Fabric, page 6, to prepare fabric and print 3" x 3" photos onto fabric. When cutting out photos, add $1/4$" seam allowance along each edge for a $3^1/2$" x $3^1/2$" square.

Note: *If you would like to put a caption on your photo, type a short description then position it along the lower edge of the photo before printing onto fabric.*

Blocks

1. Sew a 1" x $3^1/2$" gold stripe strip to opposite sides of photo. Press seams toward gold stripe. (**Diagram 1**)

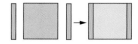

Diagram 1

2. Sew a 1" x $4^1/2$" gold stripe strip to remaining sides of photo. (**Diagram 2**) Press seams toward gold stripe.

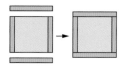

Diagram 2

3. Sew a $2^1/2$"-wide red print strip to a $2^1/2$"-wide green print strip. Press seam to one side. (**Diagram 3**)

Diagram 3

4. Cut strip set at $2^1/2$"-wide intervals. (**Diagram 4**) You will need 24 strips.

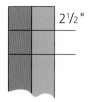

$2^1/2$"

Diagram 4

5. Sew strips to top and bottom of photo, noting position. (**Diagram 5**) Press seams away from photo.

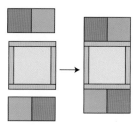

Diagram 5

6. Sew a $4^1/2$"-wide dark red strip to a $4^1/2$"-wide dark green strip. Press seam to one side. (**Diagram 6**)

Diagram 6

7. Cut strip set at $2^1/2$"-wide intervals. (**Diagram 7**) You will need 24 strips.

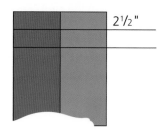

$2^1/2$"

Diagram 7

8. Sew strips to remaining sides, noting position to complete block. (**Diagram 8**) Press seams away from photo.

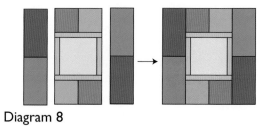

Diagram 8

9. Repeat steps 1 to 8 for remaining five more blocks.

10. Repeat steps 5 to 9, changing position of the red/green and dark red/dark green strips. (**Diagram 9**)

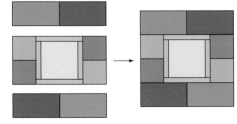

Diagram 9

Finishing

1. Place blocks in three rows of four blocks. Sew blocks together in rows. (**Diagram 10**) Press seams for rows in opposite directions; sew rows together.

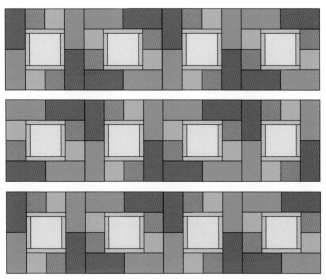

Diagram 10

2. Measure quilt lengthwise. Cut two 2^1/$_2$"-wide gold stripe strips to that length. Sew to sides of quilt. Measure quilt crosswise. Cut two 2^1/$_2$"-wide gold stripe strips to that length. Sew to top and bottom of quilt.

3. Refer to Finishing Your Quilt, pages 156 to 159, to complete your quilt.

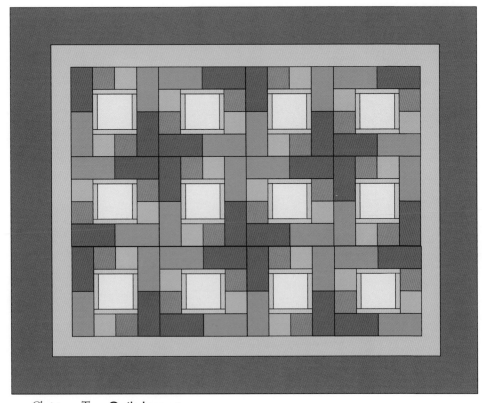

Christmas Trees **Quilt Layout**

Blazing Blossoms

Like a modern painting hanging in a museum, this quilt is sure to receive applause from all who see it. Although it looks extremely complicated, the quilt is easily made by using foundation piecing. By following the Freezer Paper Foundation Piecing instructions, the quilt can be made even faster.

Freezer Paper Technique
Foundation Piecing Method 1 or 2 (pages 7 to 14)

Approximate Size
39" x 39"

Block Size
7" x 7" finished

Materials
1 yard light green print
1 yard small pink floral
1 yard small turquoise floral
1 yard medium green print (includes first border)
$^1/_4$ yard yellow print
$^3/_4$ yard pink (includes second border)
$^1/_4$ yard blue
1 yard black floral (third border and binding)
$1^1/_4$ yard backing
Batting
Freezer Paper

Patterns
Blossom 1 (page 108)
Blossom 2 (page 109)

Cutting

Blossom Blocks

Note: *Read Foundation Piecing Methods 1 and 2, pages 7 to 14. You do not need to cut exact pieces for Method 1. For Method 2, cut the following pieces.*

16 Shape A1, yellow print
10 of each Shape A2-A6, pink
10 of each Shape A7-A10, small pink floral
10 of each Shape B1, B3, B5, B7, B9, B11, B13, B15, B17, small pink floral
10 of each Shape B2, B4, B6, B8, B10, B12, B14, B16, light green print
10 of each Shape B18-B22, medium green print
6 of each Shape A2-A6, blue
6 of each Shape A7-A10, small turquoise floral

6 of each Shape B1, B3, B5, B7, B9, B11, B13, B15, B17, small turquoise floral

6 of each Shape B2, B4, B6, B8, B10, B12, B14, B16, light green print

6 of each Shape B18-B22, medium green print

Finishing

4 strips, 1¹/₂"-wide, medium green print (first border)
4 strips, 2"-wide, pink (second border)
4 strips, 3¹/₂"-wide, black floral (third border)
4 strips, 2¹/₂"-wide, black floral (binding)

Instructions

Blocks

1. Referring to Foundation Piecing Method 1 or 2, pages 7 to 14, make ten pink Blossom blocks and six turquoise Blossom blocks. (**Diagram 1**)

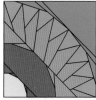

make 10   make 6

Diagram 1

Finishing

1. Place blocks in four rows of four blocks. (**Diagram 2**) Sew blocks in rows; press seams in alternating directions. Sew rows together.

Diagram 2

2. Measure quilt lengthwise. Cut two 1¹/₂"-wide medium green print strips to that length; sew to sides of quilt. Measure quilt crosswise. Cut two 1¹/₂"-wide medium green print strips to that length; sew to top and bottom.

3. Repeat step 2 for second border using 2"-wide pink strips and for third border using 3¹/₄"-wide black floral strips.

4. Refer to Finishing Your Quilt, pages 156 to 159, to complete your quilt.

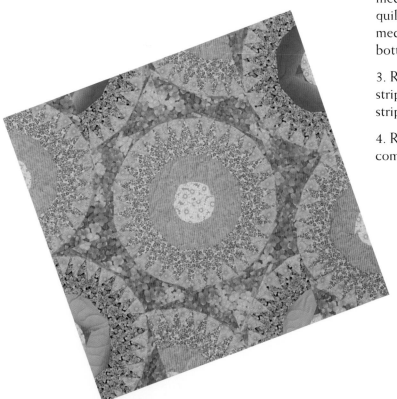

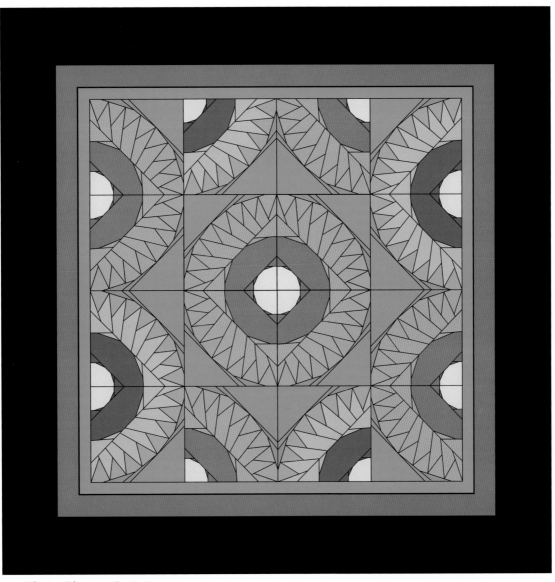

Blazing Blossoms **Quilt Layout**

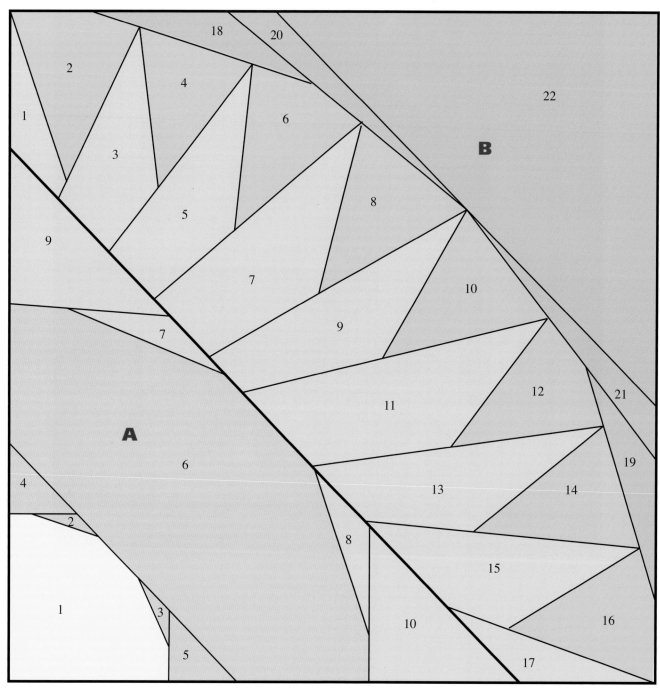

Blossom 1 Foundation Pattern

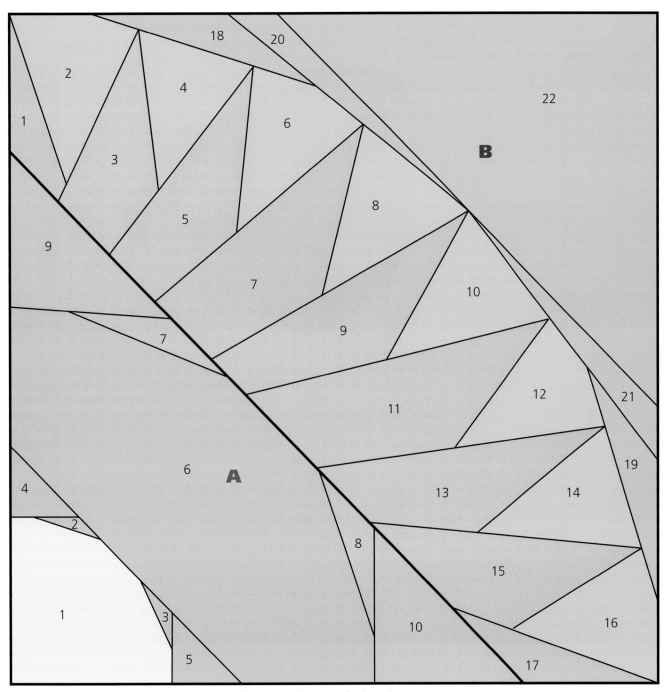

Blossom 2 Foundation Pattern

My Angel the Pug

A favorite photo of my pug, Angel, was transformed into a foundation pattern. While the quilt may look complicated, by using freezer paper and following the instructions, you too can own a pug quilt. If your pug has different coloring, feel free to use whatever colors you would like. If you don't own a pug, you should.

Freezer Paper Technique
Foundation Piecing Method 1 (pages 7 to 11)

Approximate Size
22" x 22"

Materials
Note: *The fabrics listed below and colors in the pattern pieces are suggestions only. Feel free to use fabric colors of your own that may be closer to your own lovable pooch.*

$^1/_2$ yard light blue (background)
assorted scraps of black, gray, tan, light tan, pink, and brown
$^1/_8$ yard paw print (first border)
$^5/_8$ yard black fabric (second border, binding)
1 yard backing
Batting
Freezer paper
Small piece of paper-backed fusible web
Permanent black fabric marker
White type correction fluid

Cutting
Quilt Center
Note: *You do not need to cut exact pieces for Foundation Piecing Method 1 which is the recommended technique, page 7 to 11.*

Finishing
3 strips, 2"-wide, paw print (first border)
3 strips, $2^1/_2$"-wide, black fabric (second border)
4 strips, $2^1/_2$"-wide, black fabric (binding)

Instructions

Quilt Center

1. Make foundation for patterns on pages 116 to 123 referring to Foundation Method 1, page 7 to 11.

Hints: *Some of the patterns have more than one section. Since some of those sections are small, do not cut apart until ready to sew. Write fabric choice on freezer paper pattern for each numbered shape to make piecing easier.*

2. Cut apart freezer paper sections A and B. Piece sections A and B, then sew together. (**Diagram 1**)

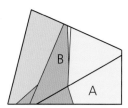

Diagram 1

3. Cut apart freezer paper sections C and D. Piece section C and D, then sew together. (**Diagram 2**)

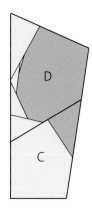

Diagram 2

4. Piece section E, then sew to A/B and C/D. This completes the lower portion of the quilt center. (**Diagram 3**)

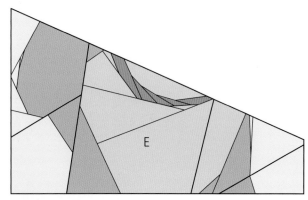

Diagram 3

5. Cut apart freezer paper sections F to M. Piece sections F, G, and H, then sew together. Piece section I, then sew to F/G/H. Piece section J, then sew to F/G/H/I. (**Diagram 4**)

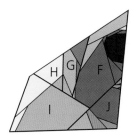

Diagram 4

6. Piece sections K, L, and M, then sew the sections together. (**Diagram 5**)

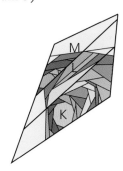

Diagram 5

7. Sew F/G/H/I/J to K/L/M. (**Diagram 6**)

Diagram 6

8. Piece section N. (**Diagram 7**)

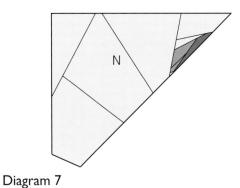

Diagram 7

9. Sew F/G/H/I/J/K/L/M/ to N. (**Diagram 8**) This completes the upper left section of the quilt center.

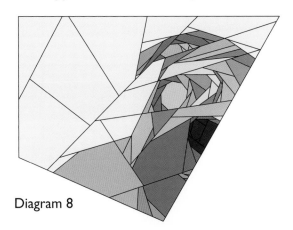

Diagram 8

10. Cut apart freezer paper sections O, P, and Q; piece the sections, then sew together. (**Diagram 9**)

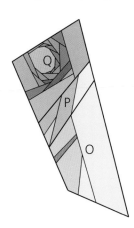

Diagram 9

11. Piece section R, then sew to O/P/Q from step 10. (**Diagram 10**)

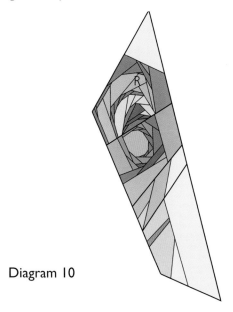

Diagram 10

12. Cut apart freezer paper sections S and T; piece the sections, then sew together. (**Diagram 11**)

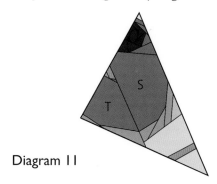

Diagram 11

13. Sew O/P/Q/R to S/T. (**Diagram 12**)

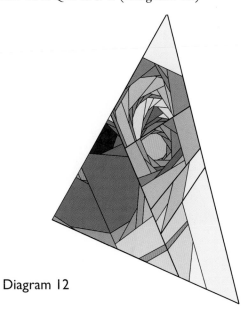

Diagram 12

14. Cut apart freezer paper sections U and V; piece the sections, then sew together. (**Diagram 13**)

Diagram 13

15. Piece section W, then sew to section U/V. (**Diagram 14**)

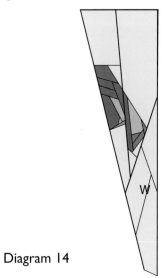

Diagram 14

16. Sew O/P/Q/R/S/T to U/V/W to complete upper right section of the quilt center. (**Diagram 15**)

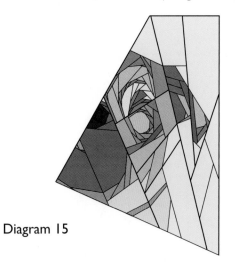

Diagram 15

17. Sew upper left section from step 9 to upper right section from step 16. (**Diagram 16**)

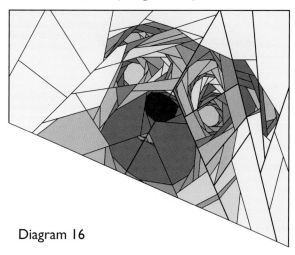

Diagram 16

18. Sew lower and upper sections together to complete quilt center. (**Diagram 17**)

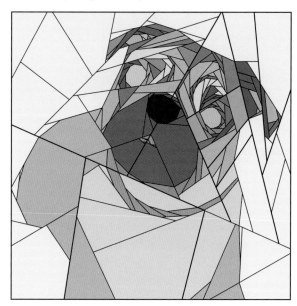

Diagram 17

19. Trace eyes from pages 119 and 121 onto paper side of fusible web. Fuse eyes on wrong side of brown fabric. Fuse to space 1 of section K and section Q. Draw pupils with permanent black fabric marker. Add a white dot using white type correction fluid. (**Diagram 18**)

Diagram 18

20. Trim quilt center ¹/4" from outside edge of freezer paper pattern. (**Diagram 19**)

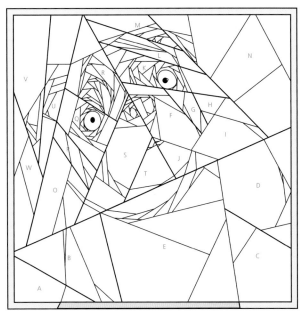

Diagram 19

Finishing

1. Measure quilt center lengthwise. Cut two 2"-wide paw print strips to that length; sew to sides of quilt center. Measure quilt center crosswise. Cut two 2"-wide paw print strips to that length; sew to top and bottom of quilt center.

2. Repeat step 1 for second border using 2¹/2"-wide black fabric strips.

3. Refer to Finishing Your Quilt, pages 156 to 159, to finish your quilt.

My Angel the Pug **Quilt Layout**

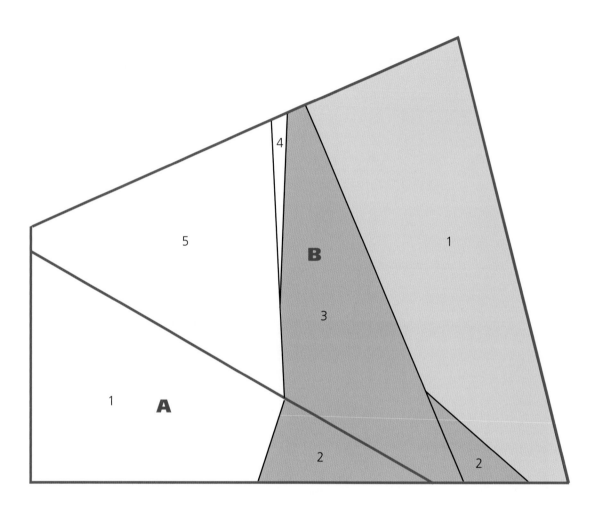

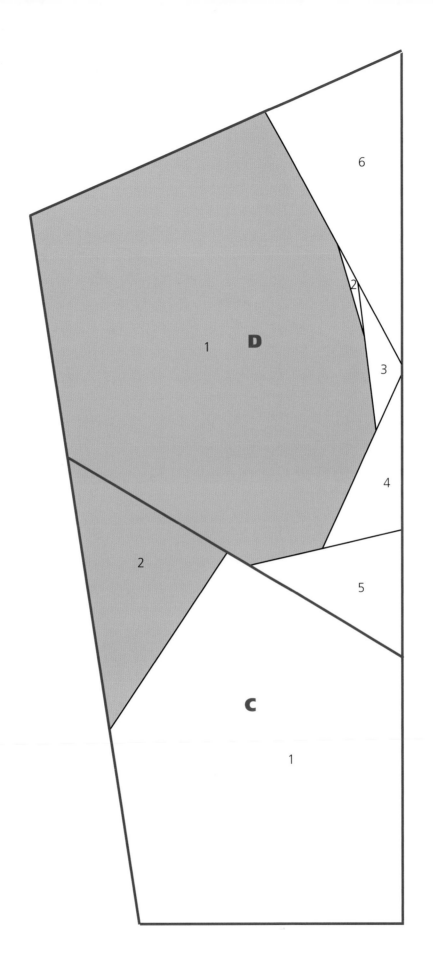

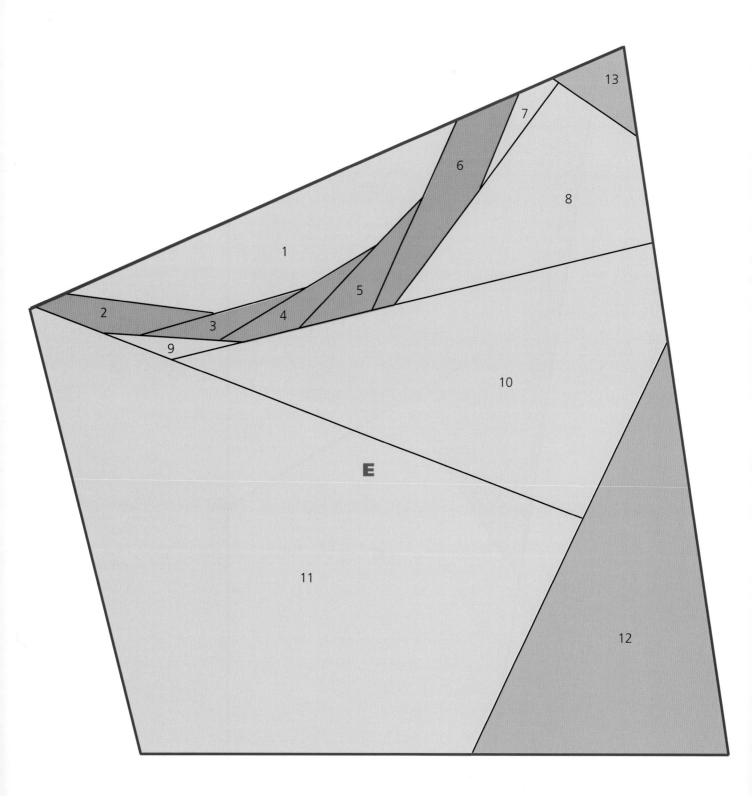

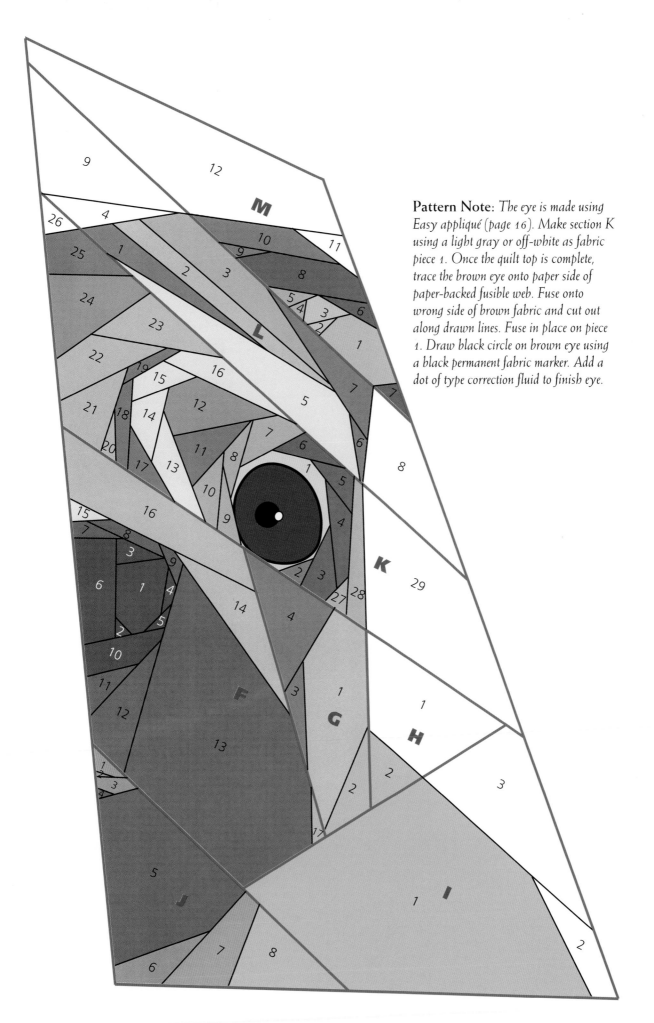

Pattern Note: *The eye is made using Easy appliqué (page 16). Make section K using a light gray or off-white as fabric piece 1. Once the quilt top is complete, trace the brown eye onto paper side of paper-backed fusible web. Fuse onto wrong side of brown fabric and cut out along drawn lines. Fuse in place on piece 1. Draw black circle on brown eye using a black permanent fabric marker. Add a dot of type correction fluid to finish eye.*

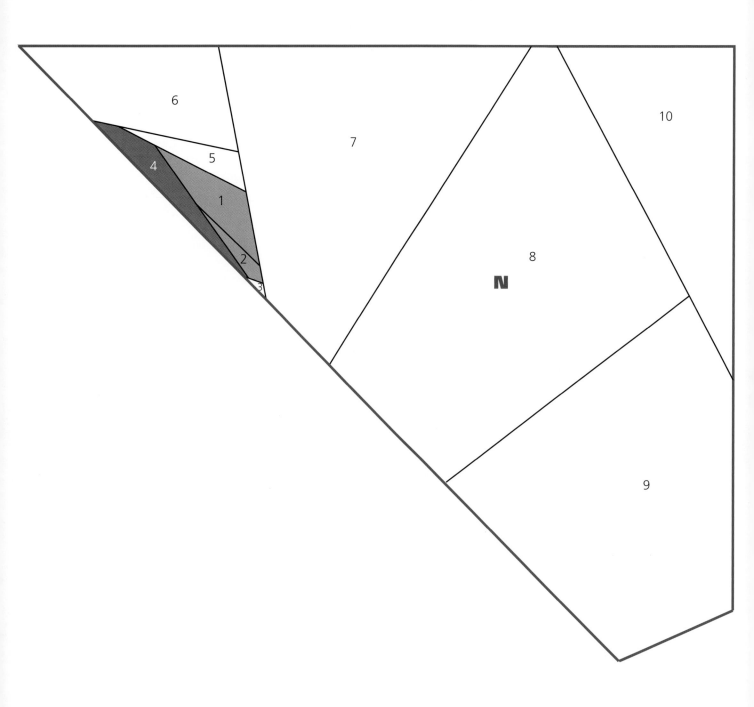

Pattern Note: *The eye is made using easy appliqué. Make section Q using a light gray or off-white as fabric piece 1. Once the quilt top is complete, trace the brown eye onto paper side of paper-backed fusible web. Fuse onto wrong side of brown fabric and cut out along drawn lines. Fuse in place on piece 1. Draw black pupil on brown eye using a black permanent fabric marker. Add a dot of type correction fluid to finish eye.*

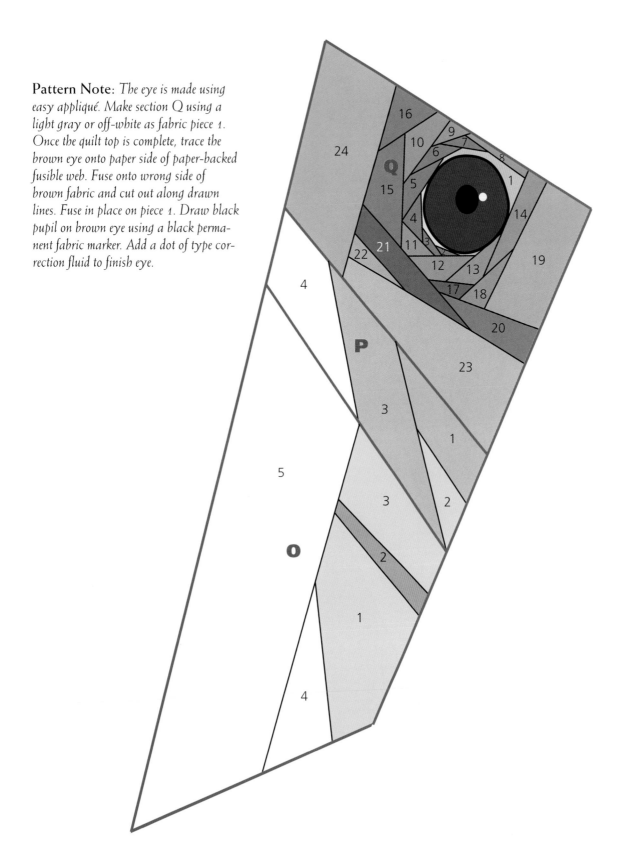

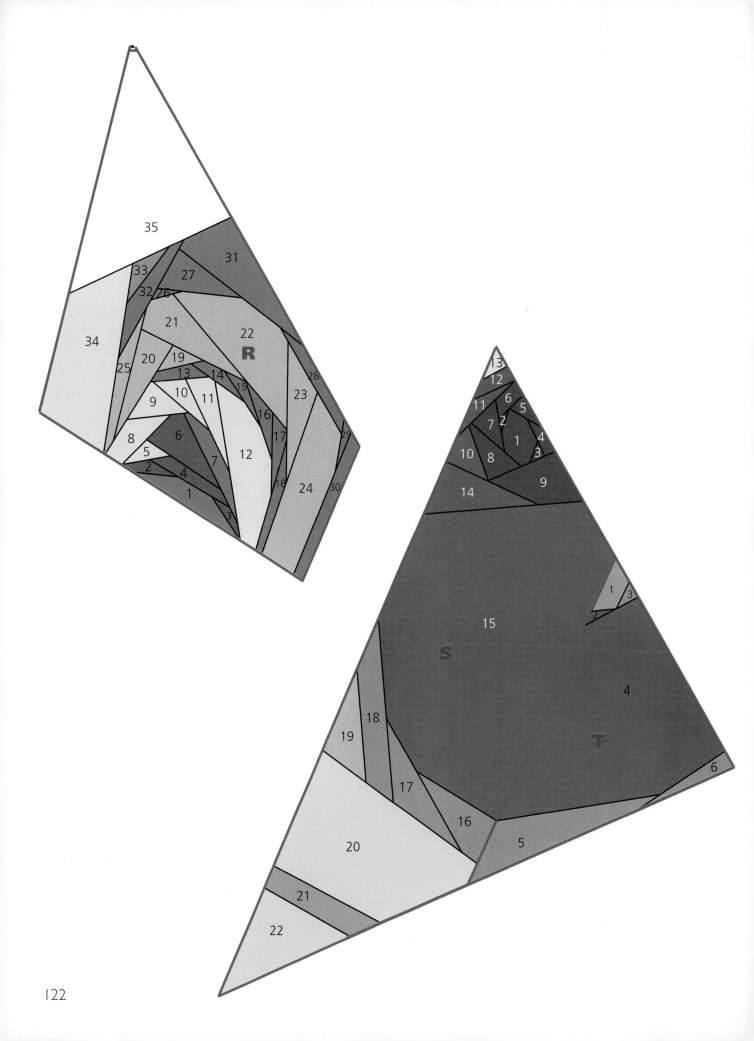

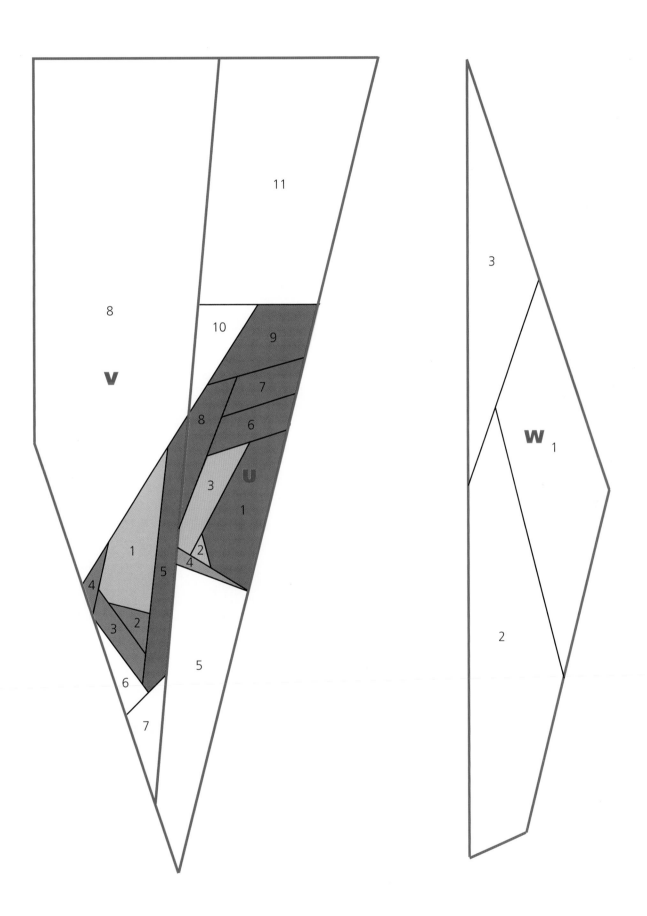

Baxter the Boxer

When my son saw My Angel the Pug Quilt (page 110), he challenged me to make a quilt from a picture of his dog, Baxter the Boxer and his favorite toy bone. Like my other doggie quilt, this one is also made using freezer paper and foundation piecing. For both doggie quilts, I was able to find a fabric with paw prints which made great borders.

Freezer Paper Technique
Foundation Piecing Method 1 (pages 7 to 11)

Approximate Size
27" x 22"

Quilt Center
20" x 15" finished

Materials
$^1/_2$ yard light blue fabric (background)
Assorted scraps of rust, brown, white, gray, black, pink, tan
$^1/_8$ yard paw print (first border)
$^5/_8$ yard brown fabric (second border, binding)
1 yard backing
Batting
White type correction fluid
Freezer paper
Permanent fabric marker

Cutting

Quilt Center
Note: *You do not need to cut exact pieces for Foundation Piecing Method 1 (pages 7 to 11) which is the recommended technique.*

Finishing
3 strips, 2"-wide, paw print (first border)
3 strips, 2$^1/_2$"-wide, brown fabric (second border)
4 strips, 2$^1/_2$"-wide, brown fabric (binding)

Instructions

Quilt Center

1. Make foundation for patterns on pages 131 to 139 referring to Foundation Method 1, pages 7 to 11. **Hints:** *Some of the patterns have more than one section. Since some of those sections are small, do not cut apart until ready to sew. Write fabric choice on freezer paper pattern for each numbered shape to make piecing easier.*

2. Cut apart freezer paper sections A to L. Piece sections A, B, and C, then sew together. (**Diagram 1**)

Diagram 1

3. Piece section D, then sew to A/B/C. (**Diagram 2**)

Diagram 2

4. Piece sections E and F, then sew together. Sew E/F to A/B/C/D. (**Diagram 3**)

Diagram 3

5. Piece section G, then sew to section from step 4. (**Diagram 4**)

Diagram 4

6. Piece sections H, I, J, and K; then sew the sections together. (**Diagram 5**)

Diagram 5

7. Sew sections from steps 5 and 6 together. (**Diagram 6**)

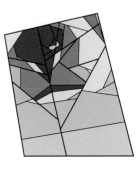

Diagram 6

8. Piece section L, then sew to section from step 7. (**Diagram 7**)

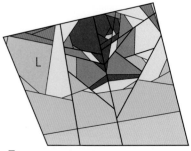

Diagram 7

9. Cut apart sections M and N. Piece M and N, then sew sections together. (**Diagram 8**)

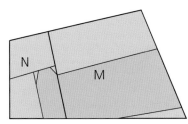

Diagram 8

10. Sew M/N to section from step 8. (**Diagram 9**)

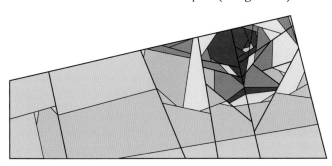

Diagram 9

11. Cut apart freezer paper sections O, P, and Q. Piece sections O and P, then sew together. Piece section Q, then sew to O/P. (**Diagram 10**)

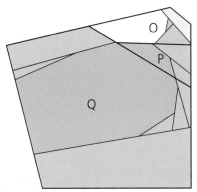

Diagram 10

12. Sew O/P/Q to section from step 10 to complete lower section. (**Diagram 11**)

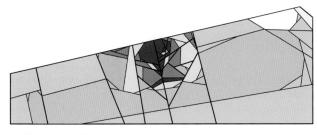

Diagram 11

13. Cut apart freezer paper sections R, S, and T. Piece sections R and S, then sew together. Piece section T, then sew to R/S. (**Diagram 12**)

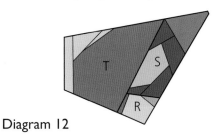

Diagram 12

14. Piece section U then sew to R/S/T. (**Diagram 13**)

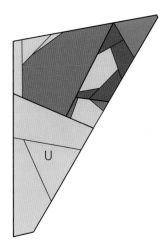

Diagram 13

15. Cut apart freezer paper sections V, W, X and Y. Piece sections V and W, then sew together. Piece sections X and Y, then sew to V/W. (**Diagram 14**)

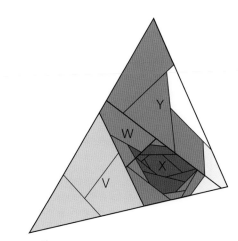

Diagram 14

16. Sew V/W/X/Y to R/S/T/U. (**Diagram 15**)

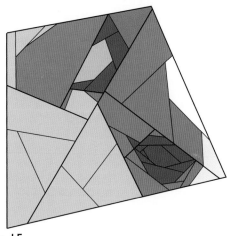

Diagram 15

17. Cut apart freezer paper sections Z and AA. Piece the sections, then sew together. (**Diagram 16**)

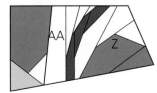

Diagram 16

18. Sew Z/AA to section from step 16 to complete upper left section of quilt center. (**Diagram 17**)

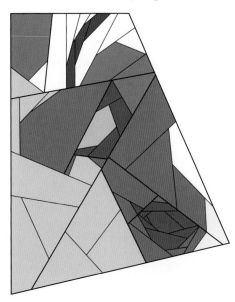

Diagram 17

19. Cut apart sections BB to FF. Piece BB to CC, then sew together. Piece DD, then sew to BB/CC. Piece EE and FF, then sew together. Sew EE/FF to BB/CC/DD. (**Diagram 18**)

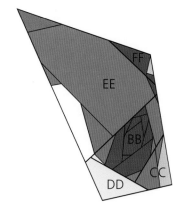

Diagram 18

20. Cut apart freezer paper sections GG, HH and II. Piece the sections, then sew together. (**Diagram 19**)

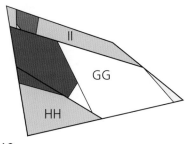

Diagram 19

21. Sew sections from steps 19 and 20. (**Diagram 20**)

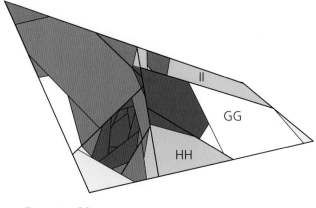

Diagram 20

128

22. Cut apart freezer paper sections JJ, KK, and LL. Piece the sections, then sew together. (**Diagram 21**)

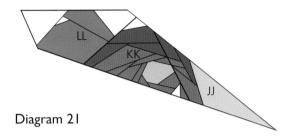

Diagram 21

23. Sew sections from steps 21 and 22 together. (**Diagram 22**)

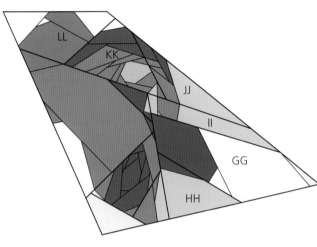

Diagram 22

24. Sew section from step 23 to upper left section from step 18. (**Diagram 23**)

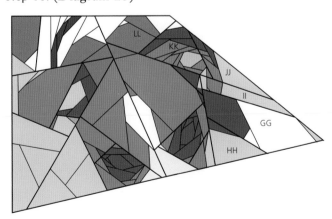

Diagram 23

25. Sew section from step 24 to lower section. (**Diagram 24**)

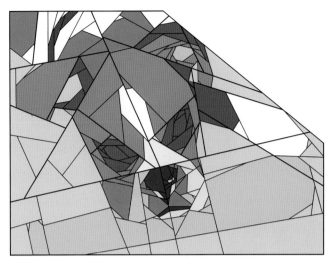

Diagram 24

26. Cut apart freezer paper sections MM and NN. Piece sections, then sew together. (**Diagram 25**)

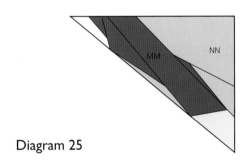

Diagram 25

27. Sew MM/NN to upper right corner to complete quilt center. (**Diagram 26**)

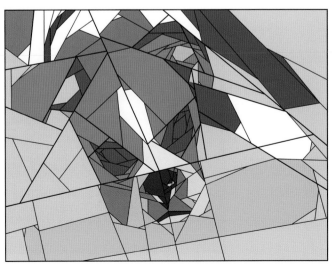

Diagram 26

28. Trace eyes and eye whites from pages 135 and 137 onto paper side of fusible web. Fuse eyes on wrong side of black fabric and eye whites on wrong side of light gray fabric. Fuse to space 1 of sections X and section BB. Add a white dot using type correction fluid. (**Diagram 27**)

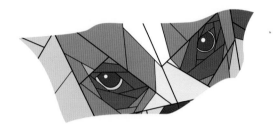

Diagram 27

29. Trim quilt center ¹/₄" from outside edge of freezer paper pattern. (**Diagram 28**)

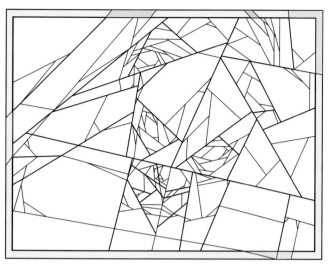

Diagram 28

Finishing

1. Measure quilt center lengthwise. Cut two 2"-wide paw print strips to that length; sew to sides of quilt center. Measure quilt center crosswise. Cut two 2"-wide paw print strips to that length; sew to top and bottom of quilt center.

2. Repeat step 1 for second border using 2¹/₂"-wide brown fabric strips.

3. Write your favorite Boxer's name on toy using a permanent fabric marker.

4. Refer to Finishing Your Quilt, pages 156 to 159, to finish your quilt.

Baxter the Boxer **Quilt Layout**

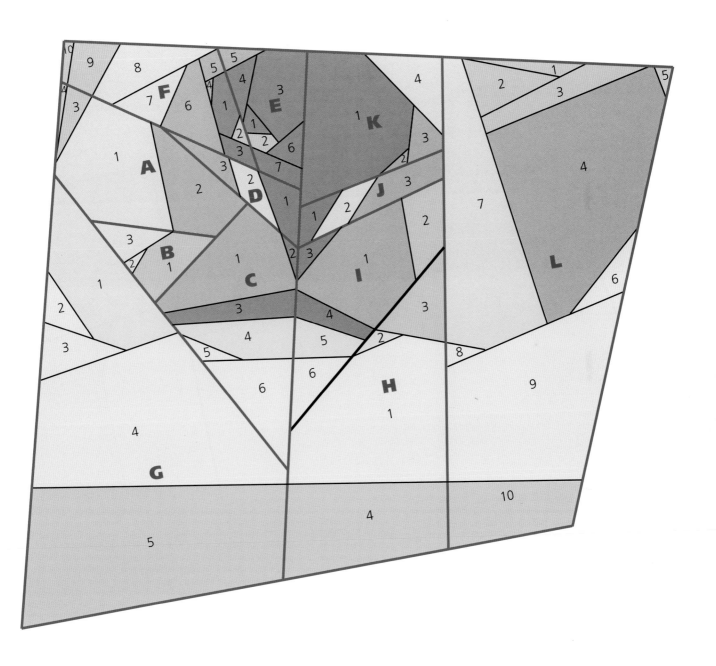

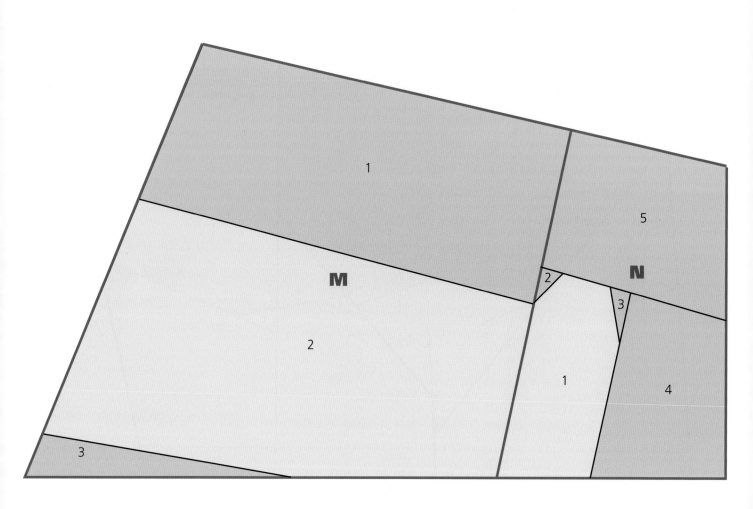

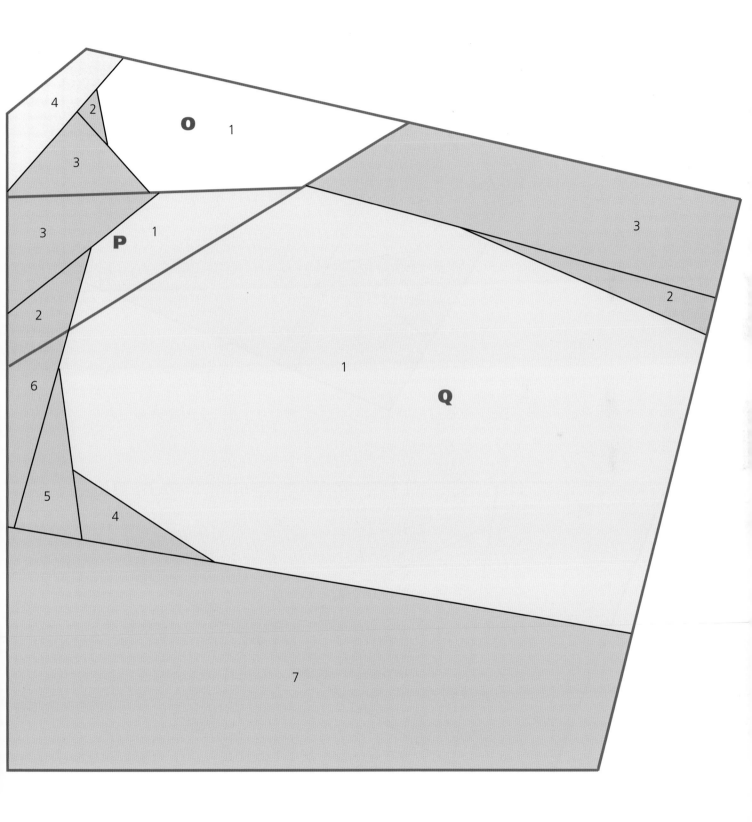

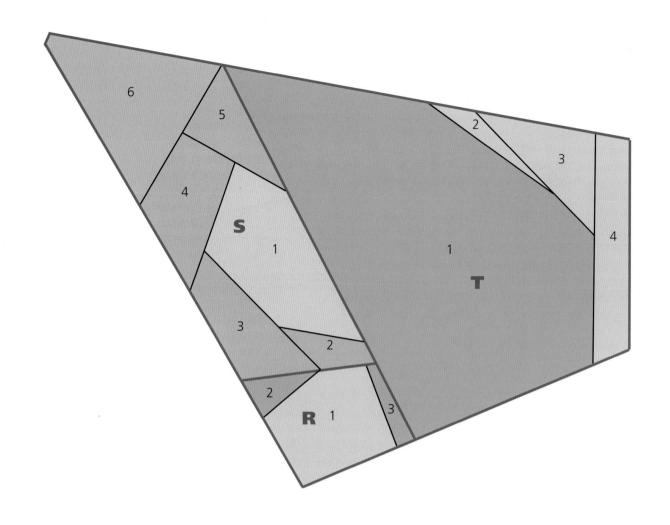

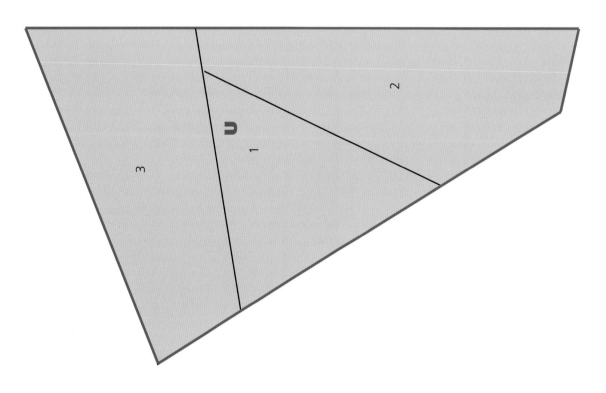

Pattern Note: *The eye is made using Easy Appliqué (page 16). Make section X using a rust as fabric piece 1. Once the quilt top is complete, trace the white and black eye parts onto paper side of paper-backed fusible web. Fuse onto wrong side of whte and black fabrisc and cut out along drawn lines. Fuse in place on piece 1. Add a dot of type correction fluid to finish eye.*

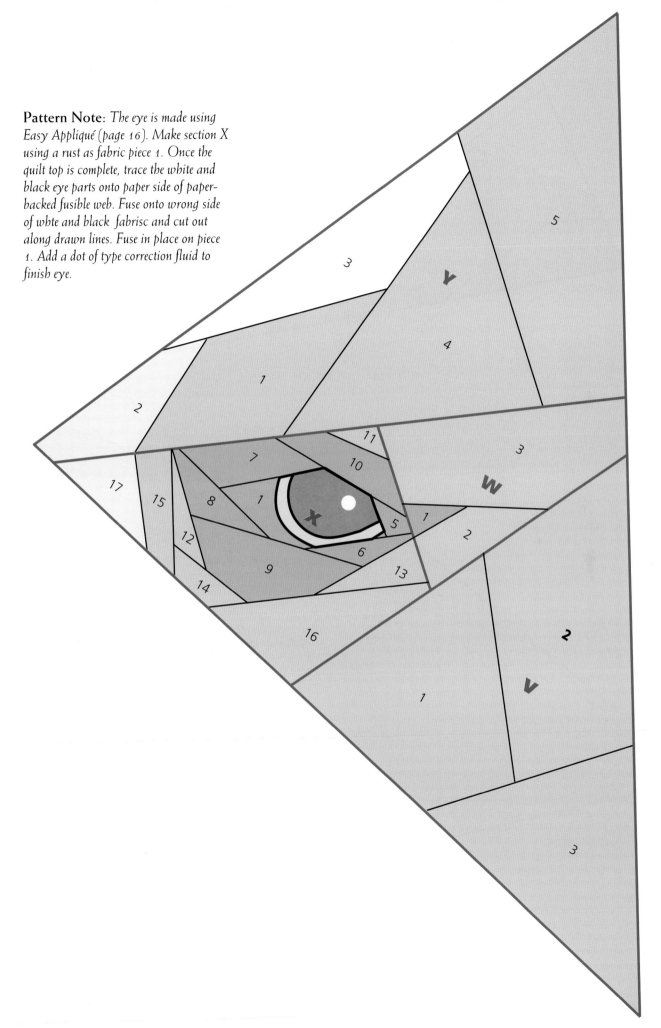

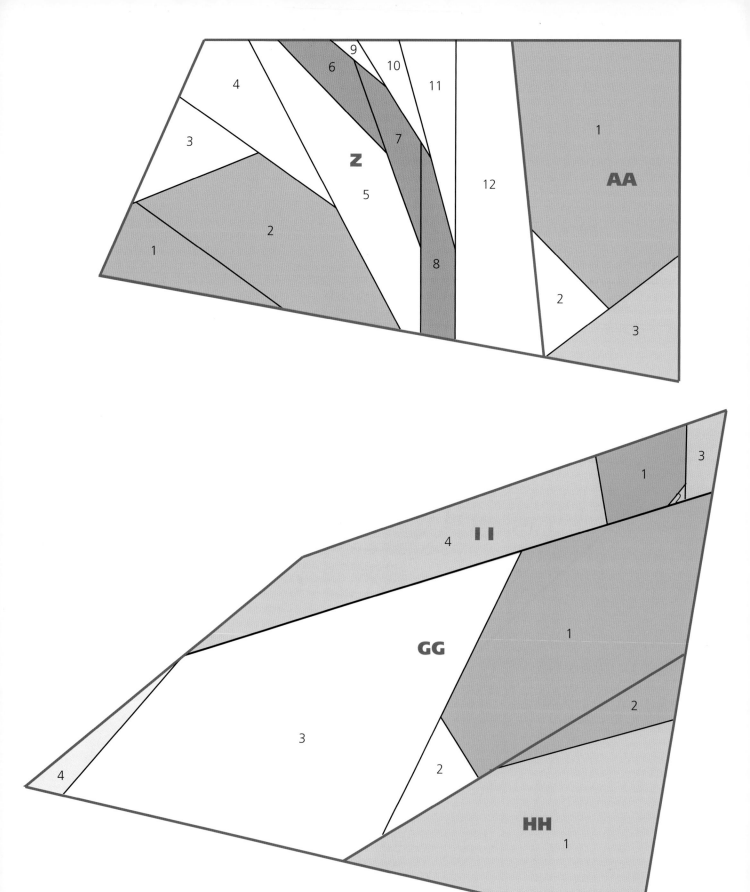

Pattern Note: *The eye is made using Easy Appliqué (pae 16). Make section BB using a rust as fabric piece 1. Once the quilt top is complete, trace the white and black eye parts onto paper side of paper-backed fusible web. Fuse onto wrong side of whte and black fabrisc and cut out along drawn lines. Fuse in place on piece 1. Add a dot of type correction fluid to finish eye.*

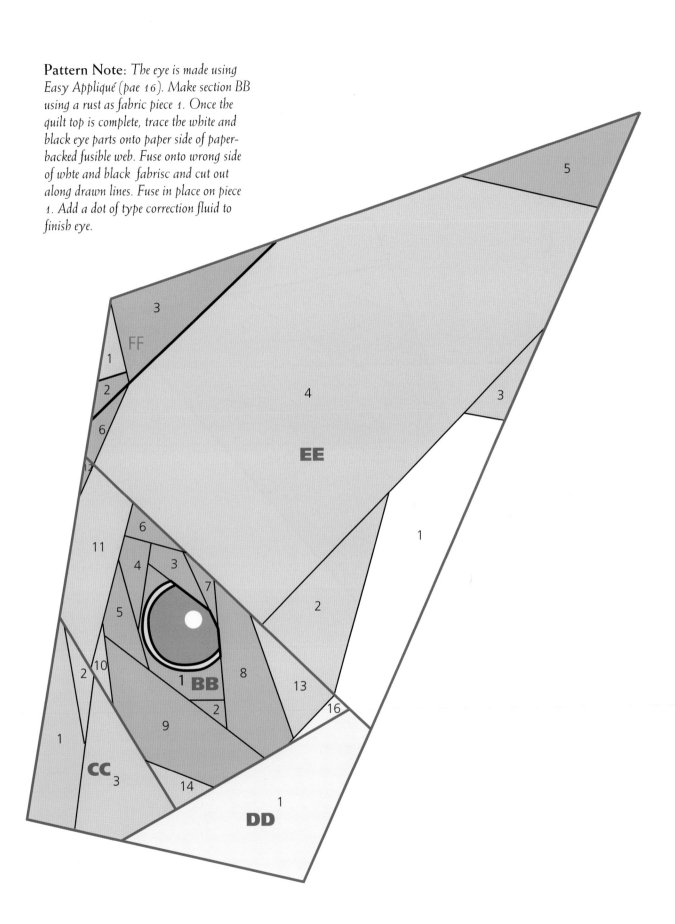

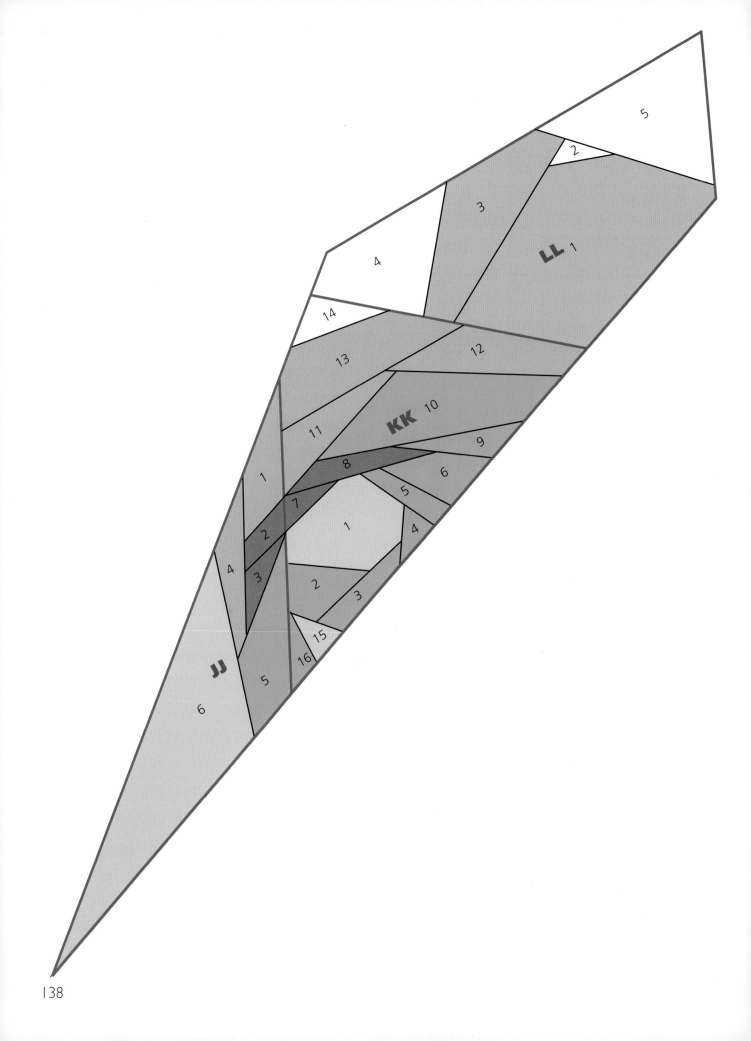

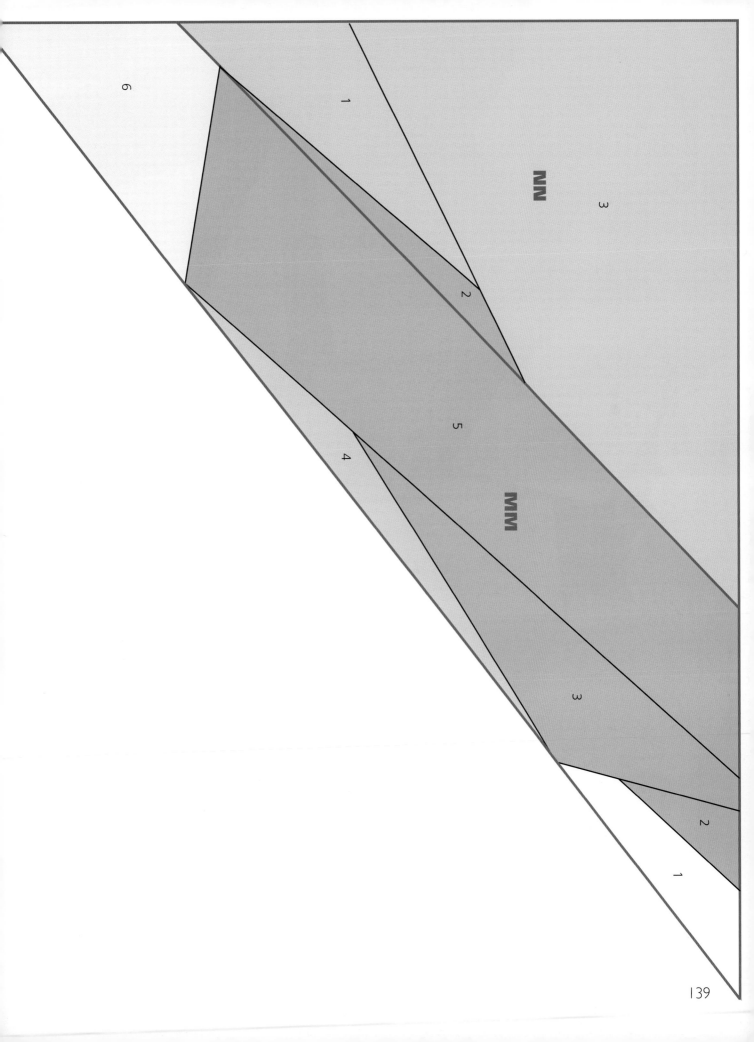

To Wanda
Happy Birthday
From Linda
August 11, 2008

Spring Garden
Hand Appliqué
Machine Quilted
Linda Causee
April 2008

To Chris and Dawn
Love and Happiness Always
Love, Mom
June 13, 2009

Flower Garden
Made in a
Learn - to - Appliqué
Workshop
April Adams
May 2008

Schoolhouse Quilt
made by
Rose Snyder
September 2008

To Kathryn
Hearts For You
Love, Mom
June 2008

To Mom
Happy Mother's Day
May 9, 2008
Love, Linda

To Evan Joseph
Welcome to this World
Love, Aunt Linda
June 5, 2008

The Finishing Touch

A quilt label is the finishing touch for your quilt. Make simple foundation-pieced blocks or blocks using easy appliqué. Then use the freezer paper to stabilize your fabric so that you can write any information about the quilt you would like the recipient to know.

Freezer Paper Technique
Writing on Fabric (page 17), Foundation Piecing (pages 7 to 14)

Approximate Sizes
Rainbow, 5" x 3^1/$_2$" finished
House, Heart, Tilted Square, 5" x 5" finished
Flowers Bugs, Flower Border, Long Stem Flowers, 4" x 6" finished
Hearts and Doves, 4" x 6" finished

Materials
Scraps of assorted colors
7" x 7" light colored fabric (background for appliqué blocks)
Freezer paper
Permanent fabric markers
Paper-backed fusible web

Patterns
Heart Foundation Pattern (page 143)
Rainbow Foundation Pattern (page 144)
House Foundation Pattern (page 144)
Tilted Square Foundation Pattern (page 145)
Flowers and Butterfly Appliqué Pattern (page 146)
Flower Border Appliqué Pattern (page 147)
Long Stem Flowers Appliqué Pattern (page 148)
Heart and Doves Appliqué Pattern (page 149)

Cutting
Foundation-Pieced Blocks
Note: *Refer to Foundation Piecing Methods 1 or 2, pages 7 to 14, to prepare pieces for cutting.*

Appliqué Blocks
Note: *Refer to Easy Appliqué, page 16, and trace patterns onto fusible web, fuse to fabric and cut out along drawn lines.*

Instructions

Foundation-Pieced Blocks

1. Refer to the Foundation Piecing Method 1 or 2, pages 7 to 14, to make your foundation from patterns on pages 143 to 145.

2. Make block of your choice. Keep freezer paper attached and write quilt information on Label block. (**Diagram 1**)

Diagram 1

3. Remove freezer paper.

4. Fold under outside edges of Label $1/4$" and press. Position label in place on back of quilt and sew in place being careful not to sew through to quilt top.

Appliqué Blocks

1. Refer to Easy Appliqué, page 16, to make Labels. Using the patterns on pages 146 to 149, cut background fabric for the block you are making $1/2$" larger in each direction. Trace pattern pieces onto paper side of fusible web; fuse onto wrong side of desired fabrics. Cut out shapes, remove paper and fuse onto background fabric. Fuse a piece of freezer paper the size of the block to wrong side of background fabric. Write quilt information on Label. (**Diagram 2**)

Diagram 2

2. Fold under outside edge of Label $1/4$"; press in place. Position Label in place on back of quilt and sew in place being careful not to sew through to quilt top.

Heart Foundation Pattern

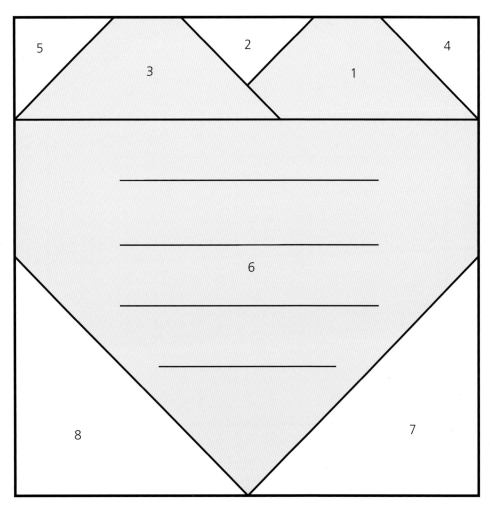

House Foundation Pattern

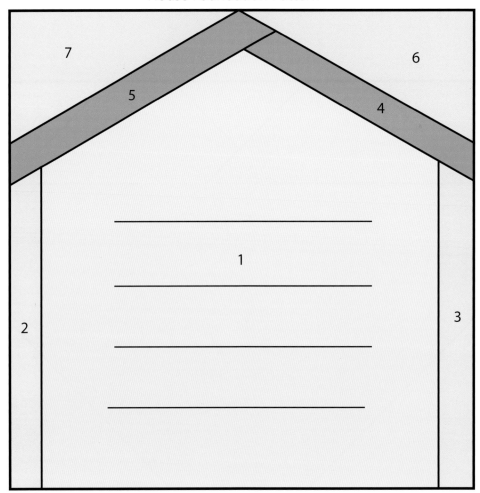

Rainbow Foundation Pattern

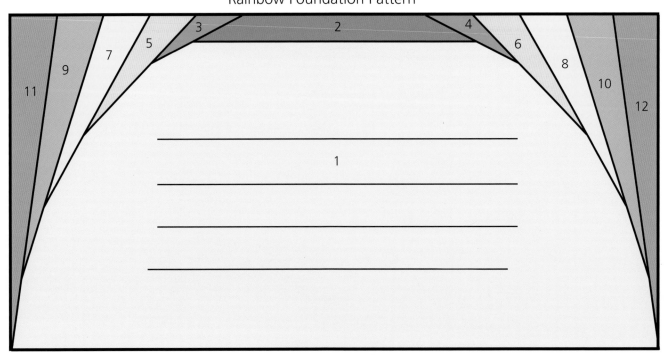

Tilted Square Foundation Pattern

Flowers and Butterfly Appliqué Pattern

Flower Borders Appliqué Pattern

Heart and Doves Appliqué Pattern

Long Stem Flowers Appliqué Pattern

General Directions

A WORD ABOUT FABRIC

For over a hundred years, quilts have been made with 100% cotton fabric, and this remains today the fabric of choice for most quilters.

There are many properties in cotton that make it especially well suited to quiltmaking. There is less distortion in cotton fabric, thereby affording the quilter greater security in making certain that even the smallest bits of fabric will fit together. Because a quilt block made with cotton can be ironed flat with a steam iron, a puckered area, created by mistake, can be fixed. The sewing machine needle can move through cotton with a great deal of ease when compared to some synthetic fabrics. While you may find that quilt artists today often use other kinds of fabric to create the quilts quickly and accurately, 100% cotton is strongly recommended.

Cotton fabric today is produced in so many wonderful and exciting combinations of prints and solids that it is often difficult to pick colors for your quilt. We've chosen our favorite colors for these quilts, but don't be afraid to make your own choices

For years, quilters were advised to prewash all of their fabric to test for colorfastness and shrinkage. Now most quilters don't bother to prewash all of their fabric but they do pretest. Cut a strip about 2" wide from each piece of fabric that you will use in your quilt. Measure both the length and the width of the strip. Then immerse it in a bowl of very hot water, using a separate bowl for each piece of fabric. Be especially concerned about reds and dark blues because they have a tendency to bleed if the initial dyeing was not done properly. If it's one of your favorite fabrics that's bleeding, you might be able to salvage the fabric. Try washing the fabric in very hot water until you've washed out all of the excess dye. Unfortunately, fabrics that continue to bleed after they have been washed repeatedly will bleed forever. So eliminate them right at the start.

Now, take each one of the strips and iron them dry with a hot iron. Be especially careful not to stretch the strip. When the strips are completely dry, measure and compare them to the size of your original strip. If all of your fabric is shrinking the same amount, you don't have to worry about uneven shrinkage in your quilt. When you wash the final quilt, the puckering that will result may give you the look of an antique quilt. If you don't want this look, you are going to have to wash and dry all of your fabric before you start cutting. Iron the fabric using some spray starch or sizing to give the fabric a crisp finish.

If you are never planning to wash your quilt, i.e. your quilt is intended to be a wall hanging, you could eliminate the pre-testing process. You may run the risk, however, of some future relative to whom you have willed your quilts deciding that the wall hanging needs freshening by washing.

Before beginning to work, make sure that your fabric is absolutely square. If it is not, you will have difficulty cutting square pieces. Fabric is woven with crosswise and lengthwise threads. Lengthwise threads should be parallel to the selvage (that's the finished edge along the sides; sometimes the fabric company prints its name along the selvage), and crosswise threads should be perpendicular to the selvage. If fabric is off grain, you can usually straighten it by pulling gently on the true bias in the opposite direction to the off-grain edge. Continue doing this until the crosswise threads are at a right angle to the lengthwise threads.

Cutting the Fabric

Although the fabric can be cut with scissors, using a rotary cutter, mat and acrylic ruler will eliminate the use of templates, as well as shorten the time spent cutting. Most importantly, rotary cutting will make cutting and piecing more accurate.

Step 1: Before cutting strips with a rotary cutter, your fabric must first be straightened. Fold fabric in half with selvages even—the cut edges may not be even at this time; fold fabric in half again with folded end even with selvages.

Step 2: Carefully place your folded fabric on the cutting mat, lining up the folded edge along one of the horizontal lines of your mat. If you are right handed, the bulk of the fabric should be to the right of the edge you are straightening; if you are left handed, it should be to the left. (**Diagram 1**)

if you are right handed

if you are left handed

Diagram 1

Step 3: Place your ruler on the fabric, lining up one of the crosswise markings of the ruler along the folded edge of the fabric; the long edge of the ruler should line up next to the cut edge. Press down firmly on the ruler and cut off the uneven edge. (**Diagram 2**)

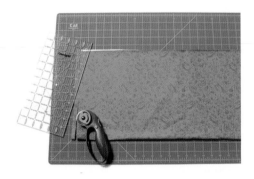

Diagram 2

Step 5: Now that you have made the initial cut, use this edge to align additional measurements. Place your ruler along the edge just straightened, lining up the correct measurement line on your ruler (the finished width of the "logs" plus ½" for seam allowance) with the straight edge of the fabric; cut your strip. (**Diagram 3**)

Diagram 3

Step 5: Once your strips are cut, you can cut squares. (**Diagram 4**)

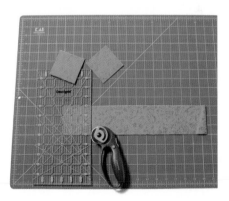

Diagram 4

Note: *Be sure that your ruler is always aligned with the folded edge as well as the cut edge of fabric*

STRIP PIECING

Strip piecing is a much faster and easier method of making quilts than creating the blocks piece by piece. With this method, two or more strips are sewn together and then cut at certain intervals. For instance, if a block is made up of several 3" x 3" finished squares, cut $3^1/2$"-wide strips along the crosswise grain. (**Diagram 5**)

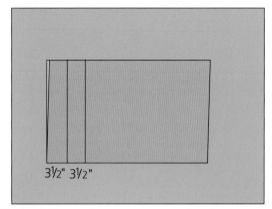

$3^1/2$" $3^1/2$"

Diagram 5

Step 1: With right sides together, sew two strips along the length. The seam should be pressed toward the dark side of the fabric. (**Diagram 6**)

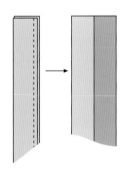

Diagram 6

Step 2: Cut across strips at $3^1/2$" intervals to create pairs of $3^1/2$" squares. (**Diagram 7**)

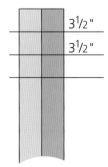

$3^1/2$"
$3^1/2$"

Diagram 7

Step 3: Sew pairs of squares to make a four patch. (**Diagram 8**)

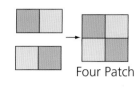

Four Patch

Diagram 8

You can sew sets of three strips together; cut across the strip sets, then sew rows together to form a nine patch. (**Diagram 9**)

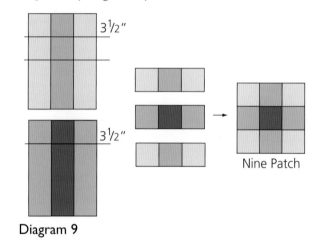

$3^1/2$"

$3^1/2$"

Nine Patch

Diagram 9

CHAIN PIECING

Chain piecing is a way to sew similar units quicky and accurately.

If you are making a project such as a quilt that has several squares that need to sewn together, you can sew pairs of squares continuously through the sewing machine without lifting your presser foot.

Step 1: Place two squares right sides together and sew along one edge using a $^1/4$" seam allowance; do not backstitch. (**Diagram 10**)

Diagram 10

Step 2: Without removing the sewn squares from the sewing machine and without lifting the presser foot, place another pair of squares on your sewing machine and continue sewing. (**Diagram 11**)

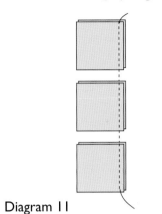

Diagram 11

Step 3: Continue sewing in this manner until all your pieces are sewn together.

Step 4: Take the entire "chain" of squares to your ironing board and press seams toward the darker fabric. Clip threads between pairs of squares.

STITCH AND FLIP

This is a method for quickly creating triangles and octagons or trapezoids. Instead of cutting these shapes, you cut and sew squares or rectangles together. (**Diagram 12**)

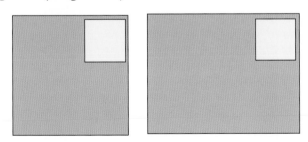

Diagram 12

Step 1: With right sides together, place a small square in the corner of a larger square or rectangle. You then sew diagonally from corner to corner of the small square. (**Diagram 13**)

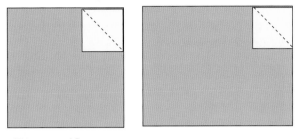

Diagram 13

Step 2: Trim the corner about ¼" from the seam line. (**Diagram 14**)

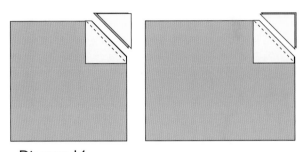

Diagram 14

Step 3: Flip the resulting triangle over and press. (**Diagram 15**)

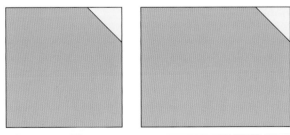

Diagram 15

Step 4: Repeat at the other corners. (**Diagram 16**)

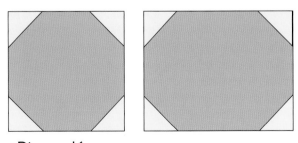

Diagram 16

BORDERS

Simple Borders

Step 1: To add your borders, measure the quilt top lengthwise and cut two border strips to that length by the width measurement given in the instructions. (**Diagram 17**)

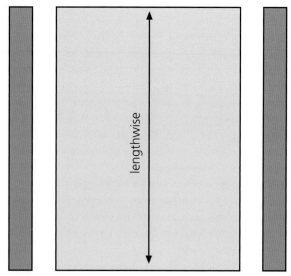

Diagram 17

Step 2: Strips may have to be pieced to achieve the correct length. To make the joining seam less noticeable, sew the strips together diagonally. Place two strips right sides together at right angles. Sew a diagonal seam. (**Diagram 18**)

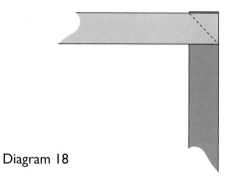

Diagram 18

Step 3: Trim excess fabric ¼" from stitching. (**Diagram 19**)

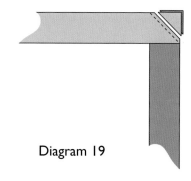

Diagram 19

Step 4: Press seam open. (**Diagram 20**)

Diagram 20

Step 5: Sew strips to the sides of the quilt. Now measure the quilt top crosswise, being sure to include the borders you have just added. Cut two border strips to that length, following the width measurement given in the instructions. Add these borders to the top and bottom of the quilt. (**Diagram 21**)

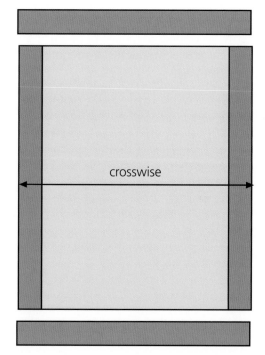

Diagram 21

Step 6: Repeat this process for any additional borders. Use the $1/4"$ seam allowance at all times and press all of the seams toward the border just added. Press the quilt top carefully.

Simple Borders With Cornerstones

Sometimes you may want to add another design element to your quilt in the form of cornerstones in the borders. They are especially useful when using a plaid fabric where it would be difficult to match the design where border strips meet. (See *Christmas Stars & Angels*, page 82)

Step 1: Measure quilt top lengthwise. Cut two border strips to that length. See Simple Borders above to piece strips to achieve the necessary length. Measure quilt top crosswise. Cut two border strips to that length. (**Diagram 22**)

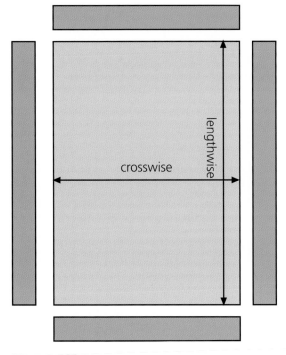

Diagram 22

Step 2: Sew lengthwise strips to the sides of the quilt. (**Diagram 23**)

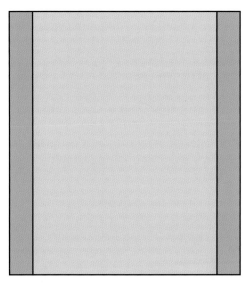

Diagram 23

Step 3: Sew squares to each end of the crosswise strips. (**Diagram 24**)

Diagram 24

Step 4: Sew to top and bottom of quilt. (**Diagram 25**)

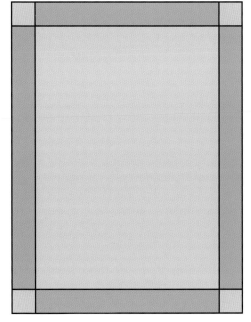

Diagram 25

FINISHING YOUR QUILT

Attaching the Batting and Backing

There are a number of different types of batting on the market today including the new fusible battings that eliminate the need for basting. Your choice of batting will depend upon how you are planning to use your quilt. If the quilt is to serve as a wall hanging, you will probably want to use a thin cotton batting. A quilt made with a thin cotton or cotton/polyester blend works best for machine quilting. Very thick polyester batting should be used only for tied quilts.

The best fabric for quilt backing is 100% cotton fabric. If your quilt is larger than the available fabric you will have to piece your backing fabric. When joining the fabric, try not to have a seam going down the center. Instead, cut off the selvages and make a center strip that is about 36"-wide and have narrower strips at the sides. Seam the pieces together and carefully iron the seams open. (This is one of the few times in making a quilt that a seam should be pressed open.) Several fabric manufacturers are now selling fabric in 90" or 108"-widths for use as backing fabric.

It is a good idea to remove the batting from its wrapping 24 hours before you plan to use it and open it out to full size. You will find that the batting will now lie flat when you are ready to use it.

The batting and the backing should be cut about one to two inches larger on all sides than the quilt top. Place the backing wrong side up on a flat surface. Smooth out the batting on top of this, matching the outer edges. Center the quilt top, right side up, on top of the batting.

Now the quilt layers must be held together before quilting, and there are several methods for doing this:

Safety-pin Basting: Starting from the center and working toward the edges, pin through all layers at one time with large safety pins. The pins should be placed no more than 4" apart. As you work, think of your quilting plan to make sure that the pins will avoid prospective quilting lines.

Thread Basting: Baste the three layers together with long stitches. Start in the center and sew toward the edges in a number of diagonal lines.

Quilt-gun Basting: This handy trigger tool pushes nylon tags through all layers of the quilt. Start in the center and work toward the outside edges. The tags should be placed about 4" apart. You can sew right over the tags, which can then be easily removed by cutting them off with scissors.

Spray or Heat-set Basting: Several manufacturers have spray adhesives available especially for quilters. Apply these products by following the manufacturers' directions. You might want to test these products before you use them to make sure that they meet your requirements.

Fusible Iron-on Batting: These battings are a wonderful new way to hold quilt layers together without using any of the other time-consuming methods of basting. Again, you will want to test these battings to be certain that you are happy with the results. Follow the manufacturers' directions.

Quilting

If you like the process of hand quilting, you can—of course—finish these projects by hand quilting. However, if you want to finish these quilts quickly, you might want to use a sewing machine for quilting.

If you have never used a sewing machine for quilting, you may want to find a book and read about the technique. You do not need a special machine for quilting. Just make sure that your machine has been oiled and is in good working condition.

If you are going to do machine quilting, you should invest in an even-feed foot. This foot is designed to feed the top and bottom layers of a quilt evenly through the machine. The foot prevents puckers from forming as you machine quilt. Use a fine transparent nylon thread in the top and regular sewing thread in the bobbin.

Quilting in the ditch is one of the easiest ways to machine quilt. This is a term used to describe stitching along the seam line between two pieces of fabric. Using your fingers, pull the blocks or pieces apart slightly and machine stitch right between the two pieces. The stitching will look better if you keep the stitching to the side of the seam that does not have the extra bulk of the seam allowance under it. The quilting will be hidden in the seam.

Free-form machine quilting can be used to quilt around a design or to quilt a motif. The quilting is done with a darning foot and the feed dogs down on the sewing machine. It takes practice to master free-form quilting because you are controlling the movement of the quilt under the needle rather than the sewing machine moving the quilt. You can quilt in any direction – up and down, side-to-side, and even in circles – without pivoting the quilt around the needle. Practice this quilting method before trying it on your quilt.

Attaching the Continuous Machine Binding

Once the quilt has been quilted, it must be bound to cover the raw edges.

Step 1: Start by trimming the backing and batting even with the quilt top. Measure the quilt top and cut enough $2^{1}/_{2}$"-wide strips to go around all four sides of the quilt plus 12".

Step 2: Join the strips end to end with diagonal seams. (**Diagram 26**)

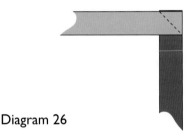

Diagram 26

Step 3: Trim the corners. Press the seams open. (**Diagram 27**)

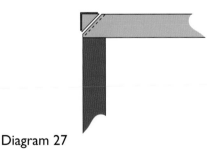

Diagram 27

Step 4: Press the seams open. (**Diagram 28**)

Diagram 28

Step 5: Cut one end of the strip at a 45-degree angle and press under $^{1}/_{4}$". (**Diagram 29**)

Diagram 29

Step 6: Press entire strip in half lengthwise, wrong sides together. (**Diagram 30**)

Diagram 30

Step 7: On the back of the quilt, position the binding in the middle of one side, keeping the raw edges together. Sew the binding to the quilt with the $^{1}/_{4}$" seam allowance, beginning about three inches below the folded end of the binding. (**Diagram 31**) At the corner, stop $^{1}/_{4}$" from the edge of the quilt and backstitch.

Diagram 31

Step 8: Fold the binding away from the quilt so it is at a right angle to the edge just sewn. Then, fold the binding back on itself so the fold is on the quilt edge and the raw edges are aligned with the adjacent side of the quilt. Begin sewing at the quilt edge. (**Diagram 32**)

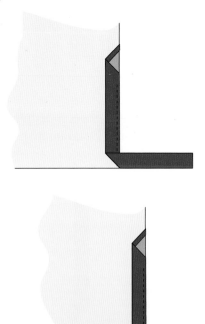

Diagram 32

Step 9: Continue in the same way around the remaining sides of the quilt. Stop about 2" away from the starting point. Trim any excess binding and tuck it inside the folded end. Finish the stitching. (**Diagram 33**)

Diagram 33

Step 10: Fold the binding to the front of the quilt so the seam line is covered; machine-stitch the binding in place on the front of the quilt. Use a straight stitch or tiny zigzag with invisible or matching thread. If you have a sewing machine that does embroidery stitches, you may want to use your favorite stitch.

Adding a Rod Pocket

In order to hang your quilt for family and friends to enjoy, you will need to attach a rod pocket to the back.

Step 1: Cut a strip of fabric, 6" wide by the width of the quilt.

Step 2: Fold short ends of strip under $^1/_4$", then fold another $^1/_4$". Sew along first fold. (**Diagram 34**)

Diagram 34

Step 3: Fold strip lengthwise with wrong sides together. Sew along raw edges with a $^1/_4$" seam allowance to form a long tube. (**Diagram 35**)

Diagram 35

Step 4: Place tube on ironing surface with seam up and centered; press seam open and folds flat. (**Diagram 36**)

Diagram 36

Step 5: Place tube on back of quilt, seam side against quilt, about 1" from top edge and equal distant from side edges. (**Diagram 37**) Pin in place so tube is straight across quilt.

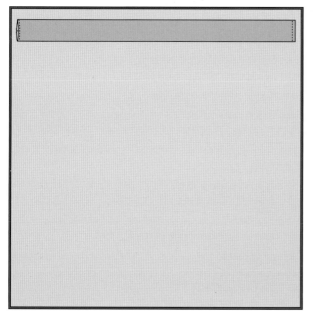

Diagram 37

Step 6: Hand stitch top and bottom edges of tube to back of quilt being careful not to let stitches show on front of quilt.

Labeling Your Quilt

Always sign and date your quilt when finished. You can make a label by cross-stitching or embroidering or even writing on a label with a permanent marking pen on the back of your quilt. If you are friends with your computer, you can even create an attractive label on the computer. See *The Finishing Touch* quilt labels, page 140, for labels you can use on your quilt.

METRIC EQUIVALENTS

inches	cm	inches	cm	inches	cm
1	2.54	11	27.94	21	53.34
2	5.08	12	30.48	22	55.88
3	7.62	13	33.02	23	58.42
4	10.16	14	35.56	24	60.96
5	12.70	15	38.10	30	76.20
6	15.24	16	40.64	36	91.44
7	17.78	17	43.18	42	106.68
8	20.32	18	45.72	48	121.92
9	22.86	19	48.26	54	137.16
10	25.40	20	50.8	60	152.40

Index